Fostoria

Serving the American Table 1887-1986

Leslie Piña

Photography
Ravi Piña

Schiffer Publishing Ltd

77 Lower Valley Road, Atglen, PA 19310

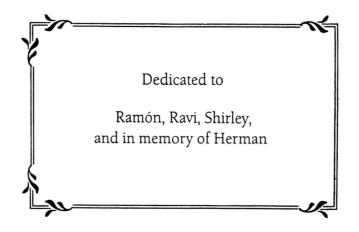

Dedicated to

Ramón, Ravi, Shirley,
and in memory of Herman

Library of Congress Cataloging-in-Publication Data

Fostoria: serving the American table 1887-1986/Leslie Piña:
photography, Ravi Piña.
    p. cm.
Includes bibliographical references and index.
ISBN 0-88740-726-9
1. Fostoria Glass Company–Catalogs. 2. Glassware–Collectors
and collecting–United States–Catalogs. 3. Glassware–United States–
History–19th century–Catalogs. 4. Glassware–United States–
History–20th century–Catalogs. I. Piña, Ravi. II. Title
NK5198.F6A4 1995
748.29154'16–dc20   94-23513
                                      CIP

Printed in Hong Kong.

Published by Schiffer Publishing, Ltd.
77 Lower Valley Road
Atglen, PA 19310
Please write for a free catalog.
This book may be purchased from the publisher.
Please include $2.95 postage.
Try your bookstore first.

We are interested in hearing from authors
with book ideas on related subjects.

Contents

Credits 4

Introduction 5

      Chronology 5

      Designers 7

Chapter 1   Victorian Pattern Glass 12

Chapter 2   American 42

Chapter 3   Coin 71

Chapter 4   Etchings and Cuttings 90

Chapter 5   Variety and Color 113

Chapter 6   Mostly Modern 156

      Labels 176

      Patterns and Decorations 177

      Glossary 191

      Select Bibliography 192

      Price Guide 194

      Index 198

Credits

One of the pleasures found in writing books is in meeting interesting and generous people who provide inspiration and encouragement as well as information and objects for photographs. Foremost on this list are Melvin Murray, author, glass historian, and curator of the Heritage Gallery, which houses the collection of the Fostoria Ohio Glass Association; and Eason Eige, author, scholar, and chief curator of the Huntington Museum of Art and his associate Linda Sanns.

Special thanks to Jon Saffell, former Fostoria mold maker, designer, and design department head, and to Fostoria's last president, Kenneth Dalzell, for sharing their time and first-hand knowledge, as well as William Litman, a third-generation Fostoria man.

I am grateful to Glenn and Betty Close and Joanne Parker, of the Fostoria Glass Society of Amertica and its Ohio chapter, for sharing their extraordinary collections, and to many others including Vicki Christensen, Mell Evers, Sharon Ferchill, Rae Hamilton, JoAn Jones, Martha MacKenzie, Robert McKeand, Kelly O'Kane, Verna Polley, Jack Ryan, Grace Wilson, Joe Gerdy of American Antiques, and Vickie Kaffeman of Second Hand Rose Antiques. Jerry Gallagher of Red Horse Inn Antiques kindly sent both objects and photographs all the way from Minnesota.

Once again, I thank Christie's, New York, for lending an auction catalog photo. I am grateful to Eleanor Moretta, director of exhibitions at Pratt Institute, and to the George Sakier Foundation for providing information . Thanks also to Terry Kovel and to Gary Schneider of the Fostoria Glass Collectors for sharing information and material, and to Lancaster Colony for kindly granting permission to use catalogs. Without libraries, there would be few new books written, and I am especially thankful for the use of : Cleveland Public Library; the libraries of Fostoria, Ohio, the Corning Museum of Glass, the Huntington Museum of Art, Ursuline College, and Ralph and Terry Kovel.

Thanks again to Paula Bloch and Shirley Friedland for proofreading, to Ramón for his help, and to our son Ravi for all the time he spent photographing glass when he would have preferred to sit at his computer (or just about anything else). And again, thanks to the staff at Schiffer Publishing for everything that they do, though it is rarely seen or understood by authors; and of course, muchas gracias to both Nancy and Peter Schiffer for being consistently terrific.

The author welcomes additional information, corrections or suggestions for future editions. Write to Leslie Piña in care of the publisher. If you would like a reply, please send a self-addressed stamped envelope.

Introduction

It is possible that more pieces of Fostoria glass have been found in kitchen cupboards, living and dining room display cabinets, and the multi-faceted American marketplace for antiques and collectibles than from any other glass company. During a century of operation, briefly in Fostoria, Ohio and then in Moundsville, West Virginia, the people who designed, crafted, and distributed Fostoria glass created an important segment of Americana and field for research and collecting. The variety of shape, pattern, decoration, and color produced by Fostoria is mind boggling. From early oil lamps and fruit jars to pressed tablesettings, from cut and etched stemware to blown art glass, Fostoria influenced and served American tastes for 100 years.

There is more than one way to deal with this variety — chronologically, stylistically, by manufacturing method, etc. One obvious category is that of late nineteenth-century Victorian pattern glass made in Fostoria, Ohio. Chapter One includes some of these earliest pressed wares. Two favorites have been the long-lived American pattern, the subject of Chapter Two, and the later entry, Coin, which is shown in Chapter Three. These are all classified and identified by a deeply pressed design that is integrated with the form. Another very important category of Fostoria is one that relies on surface decoration for its identity. Etchings were used to decorate one or more "blanks," or particular shapes, and hundreds of different intricate etchings (and cuttings) were developed to satisfy a persistent demand over the decades. A sample of these is shown in Chapter Four.

What remains is an enormous variety, a seemingly endless array of related and unrelated pieces of glass. Chapter Five explores early and late, common and rare, colorful and colorless examples. No attempt has been made to include all patterns, all colors, or all of any type — that challenge can be taken up by future researchers. Instead, a somewhat arbitrary and, I hope, interesting sample has been selected to illustrate Chapter Five. One more category, perhaps an unlikely one, is called "Mostly Modern," and is the subject of Chapter Six. These examples are shown separately, not necessarily because they do not seem to fit elsewhere, but because they warrant a place of their own in the amazing array of Fostoria designs. A lengthy, yet admittedly incomplete, list of 1,000-plus designs and decorations follows.

After a century of glassmaking, Fostoria has become a part of an enduring and endearing history. These glass objects have been handled at meals, admired as decorations, given as gifts, and passed on through generations. Perhaps partly driven by nostalgia, collectors will continue to keep the tradition alive long after the factory has closed. By adding a few pages to the Fostoria story, this book may serve to fuel that nostalgia and peak the interest of other students of Americana. The following chronology and list of designers should provide a sense of time and a glimpse at the individual personalities who stood behind the scene serving the American table.

Chronology

August 1887 - Fostoria Glass Company organizes and incorporates in Wheeling, West Virginia. Plans are made to open in Fostoria, Ohio, where free gas and a factory site are offered by the citizens of Fostoria, and about fifty skilled workers begin to locate in Fostoria. Names of early employees include mold maker Harry Humperville, Nicolas Kopp, Hayes O'Neal, Deacon Scroggins, J. F. Voitle and several from the Crimmel family - Alva C., Henry, Jacob, Jack, and Welby Crimmel. Former manager of Hobbs, Brockunier & Co. J. B. Russel becomes Fostoria's first manager. The first directors of the board are Charles E. Beam, also the first mold shop head; William S. Brady, also the first secretary; Charles Foster, engraver Otto Jaeger, and Lucien B. Martin, former Hobbs, Brockunier & Co. salesman and Fostoria's first president.

December 15, 1887 - factory begins operations. Patterns made in Ohio include salt dip No. 93, novelties such as covered animal dishes, No. 112 Cascade, No. 140 Virginia and Foster Block (same pattern), No. 141 Sterling, No. 150 Captain Kidd, No. 152 Late Icicle, No. 175 Fostoria Swirl, No. 183 Victoria, No. 200 Verona, No. 205 Artichoke, Frosted Artichoke, and Valencia (all the same pattern), No. 225 Vendome, No. 233 Ruth, No. 234 Rococo, No. 235 Olive, No. 240 Marguerite, Beaded Flange, and Fostoria Ruby. The last item number used in Ohio was No. 301 Lorraine.

1890 - Molds purchased from bankrupt Belmont Glass Co.

December 31, 1891 - Fostoria, Ohio plant closes, is purchased and immediately occupied by Seneca Glass Co. (which moves to Morgantown, WV in 1896). Otto Jaeger remains to head the Seneca Glass Co. while other executives and about sixty workers move to Moundsville.

January 1, 1892 - Fostoria Glass Co. begins in Moundsville.

1900 - blown stemware added (pressed glass was the mainstay for the first years of operation).

1901 - Lucian Martin leaves for the National Glass Co. combine; William Alexander Baxter Dalzell becomes vice-president and general manager; Willilam S. Brady becomes president for one year, then returns to being secretary.

1902 - W. A. B. Dalzell becomes president, establishes a chemical research laboratory and improves plate etching.

1924 - W. A. B. Dalzell introduces colored tableware and begins a national advertising campaign.

1925 - W. A. B. Dalzell creates special design department, offers complete dinnerware sets in glass for the first time.

1928 - Dalzell dies and Calvin B. Roe becomes president; Roe had been vice-president and secretary and Dalzell's right hand man since 1902.

1945 - Roe leaves presidency and becomes chairman of the board, remains until 1954; William F. Dalzell, son of W. A. B. Dalzell, becomes president. He had worked for the company since 1915 and was general manager in the 1920s.

1950 - company peaks with over 900 workers and 8,000,000 pieces of glass sold in more than 5,000 stores.

1958 - William Dalzell retires; Robert F. Hannum becomes president after working for the company since 1928 and serving as vice-president and general manager since 1948.

1965 - Fostoria purchases the Morgantown Glass Guild and continues to operate it until 1971.

1968 - Hannum dies and David Beaty Dalzell (son of William F.) becomes president. He joined the company in 1939, became sales manager in 1948, and served as vice-president and general manager from 1958.

1982 - David Dalzell retires and his son Kenneth B. Dalzell becomes the fourth generation of Dalzells to head the company. Kenneth started in production in 1963 and worked his way up to production manager, assistant plant manager, director of manufacturing, vice-president and general manager, and finally, president.

1983 - Kenneth Dalzell sells Fostoria to Lancaster Colony Corp. of Columbus, Ohio.

March 1986 - Fostoria plant closes.

Lancaster Colony owns the trademark and continues to operate outlet stores. Dalzell, who purchased Viking Glass of New Martinsville, West Virginia, subcontracts with Lancaster Colony to produce items of American, Coin, Argus, and other popular patterns from original molds.

Designers

One of the first Fostoria patterns, introduced when the company was still in Ohio and patented by Lucien B. Martin in 1890, is No. 183 Victoria. Curiously, it was nearly identical to a contemporary design shaded from cranberry to clear crystal made by the French firm of Baccarat and marked "Baccarat Deposée." An early Fostoria swirl pattern was also a Baccarat imitation. Two explanations are offered by Melvin Murray: first, there is evidence that several of the Fostoria workmen were originally from Alsace-Lorraine, so they might have worked at the Baccarat factory; second, Baccarat glass was being sold in the United States about the time Fostoria was beginning to create its own identity, so a piece was used as a model. (Murray 1992, 48) In either case, it is clear that glass designs used by one firm were readily copied by others. In addition to borrowing from overseas, it was common practice for American glasshouses to copy or adapt patterns from one another in order to keep up with current fashions and consumer needs. It was also common for workers to move from glasshouse to glasshouse throughout their careers, thus contributing to the spread of designs in their repertoires.

Long before artist-designers were hired to invent new shapes and patterns, the mold shop foreman usually filled this role and the glassworkers improvised changes on utilitarian wares. At Fostoria, the earliest designs were probably the creation of mold maker Charles E. Beam, who later worked for the Indiana Tumbler and Goblet Company in Greentown, Indiana and the Kokomo Glass Company in Kokomo, Indiana. (Murray 1972, 12) The first person to devote most of his time to designing Fostoria glass was Edgar Bottome, who arrived in 1897.

Edgar Bottome After leaving Lenox Glass, Bottome was hired by Fostoria in 1897 as an artist decorator. In addition to executing decorations on the glass, he began to supervise others and is considered to be the first designer. He designed plate etchings 277 Vernon, 278 Versailles, 279 June, 280 Trojan, 284 New Garland, and 327 Navarre. Although he may not have met George Sakier, these two designers were responsible for the 2496 Baroque and 2545 Flame patterns. According to Barbara Adt (1992, 6), Bottome designed the Baroque table service consisting of plates, stemware, serving items, and punch bowl.

Phillip Ebeling Originally from Findley, Ohio, Ebeling came to serve as foreman in the moldmaking department at Fostoria in 1901. He

designed glassmaking machinery and patented several designs for molded glass, notably the American pattern in 1915. His visits to European glasshouses undoubtedly influenced his work. Ebeling's other patents include a line of molded and intaglio cut wares with floral motifs in 1904, glass tops for shakers in 1908, candle lamps in 1912, and three similar patterns: 1913 Flemish, 2106 Vogue, and 2222 Colonial. (Adt July & Dec 1993) These were among the models for the later Coin pattern, making Ebeling directly or indirectly responsible for Fostoria's two most popular patterns.

William H. Magee In 1928 he designed 2380 candy jar and cover, 2394 2-in. candle, 2398 11-in. bowl, and 5298 stem (1928-31).

Marvin Yutzey A graduate of the Cleveland School (Institute) of Art, Yutzey worked for Halle Bros. department store in Cleveland before joining Fostoria in 1936. He began working under Bottome and also worked closely with contracted designer George Sakier. Since outside designers often sent in only concept designs, it was up to Yutzey and other in-house designers to adapt them to the glassmaking process. Eventually, Yutzey became the first director of design at Fostoria. He designed 2630 Century; the 6097 Sheraton shape; 2864 ashtrays and coasters in 1973; 2885 Stratton 24% lead crystal pressed barware and stemware in 1973; 2887 Heritage crystal barware and stemware; lead

crystal Christmas ornament series with 2901 Snowflake, 2902 Holly, 2927 Christmas Tree, 2928 Wreath, 2964 Christmas Sphere, and 2965 Bell; 2907 Grace bud vase; 2908 Melissa bud vase; 2919 Salem shaker in 1975; 2969 picture frames; 2973 Revere shaker; and American Milestones commemorative plates, States plates, and Old Glory series in collaboration with Jon Saffell. Yutzey retired in 1977.

Robert Cocanhougher Developed carvings from 1938 to 1942.

Fernando Alvarez Joined Fostoria in 1939 and worked closely with design director Yutzey. Because of his diplomacy and easy manner, Alvarez acted as a liaison between the design department, mold shop, and factory. He became design department manager in the 1960s and took over more of the technical duties, leaving Yutzey more creative time. The blown iron mold Mesa pattern and 6125 Distinction were Alvarez designs, as were 2882 Moonstone and the 2821 animal series consisting of bear, bird, cat, dolphin, owl, penguin, and turtle. He was involved with many other designs and sometimes developed the concepts of outside designers. For example, Sakier sometimes sent in what Ken Dalzell calls "three squiggles on tissue paper" which Alvarez and Yutzey then adapted to the glass medium. He died in 1972.

Robert Grove Graduating from the Carnegie Institute of Technology, Grove came to Fostoria in 1950 but stayed only six months.

Fred Yehl Left a teaching position at Auburn University to work with Yutzey and Alvarez in 1952 and stayed until 1957.

Jon Saffell Straight from Moundville High in 1957, Saffel began as a mold maker in the design department. While working with and learning from Yutzey and Alvarez during the day, he attended evening classes at West Liberty State College. His first designs were the novelties 420 frog and 452 ladybug in 1970. When Greg Pettit was hired as a model maker in 1971, Saffell gained more creative

time and designed the first 24% lead crystal cutting 916 and 935 Greenfield and the pressed pattern 2936 Transition. Alvarez died suddenly in December 1972, and Saffell was made design department manager. Pettit, Yutzey, and Saffell worked as a team and produced 555 American Milestones, 2860 Panelled Diamond Point, and many others. Since Saffell was the model maker for many new designs, he participated in the design development going on at the time and worked on a good deal of stemware with Sakier. He became design director in 1977 when Yutzey retired and remained until the closing in 1986.

Greg Pettit Hired in 1971 as a model maker for the design department, Pettit became one of the Yutzey-Saffell team and made masters for the mold shop in addition to designing.

William Hoffer A graduate of Kent State University, Hoffer designed for Fostoria from 1974 to 1979.

William Bradford While attending West Virginia University, Bradford worked part time for Fostoria and joined the design department in 1976. Most of his work involved two-dimensional design such as art work for etching plates.

Judy Olert New product suggestions were the main task of the product development department, which Olert headed in the 1980s.

In addition to regular full-time designers, others were contracted on a consultant basis as were students from the Philadelphia School of Art and Carnegie Mellon in their work/study programs. These free-lance designers worked under various arrangements: retainer, in which a regular monthly stipend was paid to retain the designer; royalties, where a percentage of sales was paid to the designer; outright purchase, a less common practice whereby Fostoria purchased the design and all rights to it; and a combination of retainer and royalties. (Dalzell interview) Among the more prominent names were:

George Sakier Born in 1897 in Brooklyn, New York, Sakier studied at Pratt Institute and Columbia University. An industrial and product designer and

an oil painter, he exhibited at the Metropolitan Museum of Art, Museum of Modern Art, Philadelphia Museum of Art, (Falk 538-39) and the Louvre. He also designed theme exhibits at the 1939 New York World's Fair, directed the Municipal Art Society of New York City, and served with the Army Camouflage Division in World War I and as a research engineer in World War II. In 1944 he and thirteen other designers chartered the Society of Industrial Designers; in 1947 Sakier headed the education committee of the organization. (Pulos 180 & 200) Sakier was art director for *Harper's Bazaar* from 1927 to 1929, and then in 1929 he began a relationship with Fostoria. Eventually Sakier took up residence in Paris, where his interests focused on oil painting, especially abstract designs in vivid colors, and he also had a studio on Long Island. Although most of his designs were sent in, he sometimes came to Moundsville for four or five-day visits and stayed with the William F. Dalzells. (Dalzell interview)

His designs include the 2404, 2409, and 2428 Lotus series of Art Deco mold blown vases; stemware 6011 Classic including the Whirlpool 730

cutting; stemware 6017, 6027 Envoy, and 6030; some items of 2412 Colony; items in both the 2484 and 2496 Baroque pattern; 2594 candlesticks; 2638 candlestick; 2639 duo candlestick; in 1958 both the 2718 Fairmont pattern and 2719 Jamestown pattern; 2746 pressed Chinese ashtray; 2747 and 2748 ashtrays; the 2749 Windsor, 2750 Hapsburg, and 2751 Navarre of the Crown Collection of the late 1950s; 2760 which included a 5 1/2-in candlestick; 2761 and 2762 candlesticks; 2763 10-in. candlestick with a twisted column similar to Colony; 2764 and 2765 candlesticks; 2766 Luxembourg Crown; 2767 candlestick; 6113 Versailles blown crystal stemware with 683 gold decoration on the stem in 1969; and 2832 Sorrento in 1976, an intentionally crude knock-off of a Franciscan design. When Fostoria closed in 1986, he was still sending designs from his home in Paris. Sakier died in 1988.

Raymond Loewy French born, major American industrial designer known for modern Streamlined style, Loewy was responsible for such diverse designs as the S-1 bullet-shaped locomotive, Greyhound Scenicruiser coach, Studebaker Champion and Avanti, Sears Coldspot Super Six refrigerator, Lucky Strike cigarette package, logos for British Petroleum, Exxon, and Shell Oil companies, and the NASA Skylab interiors. (Eidelberg 384) In 1944 he was a charter member of the Society of Industrial Designers (along with other Fostoria designers, George Sakier and Russel Wright). He designed Fostoria's 2700 Radiance pattern, which was a total failure, because a cheap machine-made version had been made by another company. Unfortunately, a very large run was produced, because Fostoria expected the pattern to be a big success. According to Ken Dalzell,"every church in Marshall County had Radiance, because people gave it away."

Russel Wright Another twentieth-century American designer, known for everything from Steubenville's American Modern dinnerware to blonde furniture, Wright was a major force in introducing modern design into the American home. His seed glass plates and bowls designed for Fostoria from 1946 to 1948 were never produced commercially.

Ben Seibel Besides his work for Mikasa, Seibel designed Impromptu and Informal patterns for Iroquois China shortly after Wright designed his Iroquois Casual. Although he resided in Greenwich Village in New York City, Seibel was an important Fostoria designer, especially during the 1950s. He designed 2762 Facets in the 1950s; 6108 Precedence in 1967; 2806 Pebble Beach in 1969; 2824 Module in 1971; 2826 and 2827 centerpieces with candleholders; 2829 and 2830 candy jar and candy box; 6126 Corsage Plum in 1973; 2903 Monarch lead crystal in 1974; 2926 Gourmet in 1976; 2934 York lead crystal barware and stemware and 2937 candle bud vase in 1976.

Monarch
Lead Crystal Stemware and Barware

Double Old Fashioned, High Ball, Dessert, Goblet, Wine, Luncheon Goblet/Ice Tea

Helena Tynell Glass designer from Finland who met David Dalzell when he was in Europe. Tynell designed for the Riihimáki glassworks in Finland, preferring an abstract organic style using simple shapes often with optical distortion (Eidelberg 156) She created Fostoria's 2825 and 2844 Seashell pattern; 2842 and 2856 Serendipity giftware line; 2868 Family paperweights; and 2842 candle ashtray, a freeform design with tapered bottom and glass swelling up over the top like a mushroom, all in the 1970s.

James Carpenter Studio glass blower and designer for Steuben, Carpenter came to Fostoria for the 1977-78 year to develop the "Designer Collection" of blown art glass. The 28 shapes were divided into four groups and named Images, Interpretations, Impressions, and Impromptu, usually with a signature and date engraved on each piece. Carpenter later started a company in New York City called Design Associate Inc. (Ziegler 70)

According to Jon Saffell, the ideal design process as it was in 1983 might look like this:

1. Need - product development and market research identify need
2. Design strategy - "need" begins creative sessions with design department
3. Creative sessions - in house and consultant designers brainstorm
4. Preliminary design - rough sketches by design department
5. Creative session II - critique by design department and product development
6. Focused design - models by design department
7. Consumer research - all of above departments participate
8. Refine designs - design department
9. Decision - company executives
10. Production - final drawings, masters, molds, samples approved for production

Much of the information about designers is from an article written by Jon Saffell in 1983 and an interview with him in 1994.

Chapter 1

Victorian Pattern Glass

During the early years in Fostoria, Ohio, the company was like many other nineteenth-century glasshouses in America. Pressed pattern glass was what Fostoria and others advertised in the trade journals and what they sold to consumers. Some of the Victorian items — molasses cans and spooners, or spoons — would eventually be phased out, but the basis for their production and the market to which they were aimed would continue. Table and decorative wares suited for middle class domestic use and for wedding gifts would be Fostoria's mainstay for nearly a century.

Consistent with the times and needs, this early production also included a range of oil lamps, pressed with the same patterns in the same late Victorian styles as the table items. Most of the glass was colorless, though some color was occasionally used. The term crystal is used to describe the colorless clear glass, but it did not contain lead, so it should not be confused with lead crystal. Frosting or etching, to give the surface a matte finish, was a common decorative technique during the early years, and some patterns were available in both a glossy finish and one with a combined glossy and matte finish. The early glass was often thicker and heavier than much of the later product; the No. 272 footed vase, for example, was extremely thick and heavy. These patterns were phased out as styles changed and as color came into favor in the 1920s.

Because this Victorian pattern glass can be distinguished from Fostorias later pressed glass styles, and certainly from the delicately blown and cut wares, and because it was often discontinued relatively soon after its introduction, it should be fairly easy to identify. However, some patterns were reintroduced, sometimes under new names. Cascade returned as Queen Anne and as Colony, and these new issues were produced for a much longer time than the nineteenth-century originals. Where glass is concerned, nothing is ever easy. But the challenges of identifying, not to mention finding, this early pattern glass are among the ingredients that give collecting its flavor.

Although some of the earliest pressed patterns were also made in Moundsville, beginning in 1892, numbers up to 301 are considered to be Fostoria, Ohio production. The 1891 catalog includes nineteen of these: 97, 112, 140, 150, 162, 175, 183, 184, 187, 200, 205, 225, 226, 233, 234, 235, 240, 255, and 301; several are pictured in this chapter.

1.1 Fostoria Glass Company paperweight made in Fostoria, Ohio and dated 1891, L. 4 1/2 in. *Collection and courtesy of Fostoria Ohio Glass Association*

1.2 Fostoria Glass Co. stock certificate dated 1902 and signed by W.A.B. Dalzell. *Collection and courtesy of Fostoria Ohio Glass Association*

1.3 Leaded glass logo above the entrance to the Heritage Gallery which houses the collection of the Fostoria Ohio Glass Association in Fostoria.

1.4 Display of early Fostoria glass in the Heritage Gallery showing several pieces of the No. 183 Victoria pattern and the colored Baccarat piece that inspired No. 112 Cascade, the pressed pattern introduced in 1888.

1.5 Display of early Fostoria glass in the Heritage Gallery with several pieces of No. 112 Cascade.

1.6 Display of early Fostoria glass in the Heritage Gallery showing No. 183 Victoria.

1.7 Glass paperweight made by Fostoria Glass Co. for the Isaac Harter Co. L. 4 1/2 in. *Collection and courtesy of Fostoria Ohio Glass Association*

1.8 Neighboring Fostoria Barrel and Stave Co. made the oak base for this Fostoria desk set in Cascade, about 1888. W. 11 in., H. 5 5/8 in. *Collection and courtesy of Fostoria Ohio Glass Association*

1.9 Cascade, the first Fostoria pressed tableware pattern, was illustrated in the May 17, 1888 issue of *Pottery and Glassware Reporter*; it was reissued as 2412 Queen Anne and 2412 Colony and then in 1982 as the colored 6149 Maypole; 9-inch Cascade candlesticks and glass jar mounted with metal base, lid, and handle, H. 11 in., circa 1890. *Collection and courtesy of Fostoria Ohio Glass Association*

112 Candlestick.
Packed 4½ doz. in bbl.

1.10 Cascade candlestick with counter clockwise swirl; early advertisements and catalog illustrations show the swirl going both counter clockwise and clockwise. *Courtesy Second Hand Rose Antiques*

1.11 Cascade candlestick from 1901 catalog.

1.12 Cascade pattern circa 1890; left, small cruet, H. 4 1/2 in.; center, honey pitcher, H. 4 1/2 in.; right, cruet, H. 9 5/8 in. *Collection and courtesy of Fostoria Ohio Glass Association*

1.13 Cascade flasks circa 1890; left H. 6 in.; right H. 7 3/4 in. *Collection and courtesy of Fostoria Ohio Glass Association*

1.14 Cascade full-patterned stoppered jug, H. 7 3/4 in., with half-patterned jug circa 1890. *Collection and courtesy of Fostoria Ohio Glass Association*

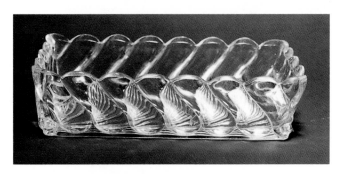

1.15 Cascade rectangular dish, L. 7 in. *Collection and courtesy of Fostoria Ohio Glass Association*

1.17 Pressed pattern No. 140 is called both Foster Block and Virginia and is made up of hexagons and triangles, which when viewed together become six-pointed stars; one of the earliest patterns, it was illustrated in the Dec. 27, 1888 issue of *Pottery and Glassware Reporter*, decanter, H. 8 in. *Collection and courtesy of Fostoria Ohio Glass Association*

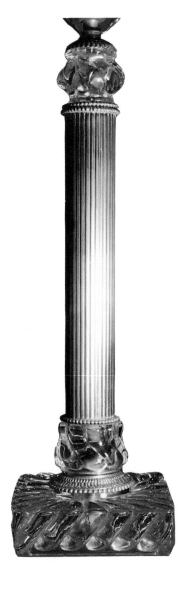

1.18 Left, No. 140 Virginia/Foster Block cruet, H. 7 1/2 in.; right, two-handled covered jar, H. 6 in. *Collection and courtesy of Fostoria Ohio Glass Association*

1.16 Cascade/Colony lamp base.

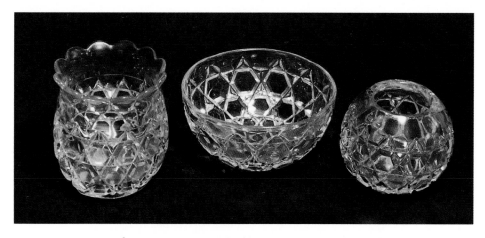

1.19 Left, Virginia/Foster Block spooner or spoon with flared and scalloped top; center, small bowl with straight top; right, 3 1/2-in. rose bowl. *Collection and courtesy of Fostoria Ohio Glass Association*

1.20 Virginia/Foster Block 8-in. bowl with scalloped top. *Collection and courtesy of Fostoria Ohio Glass Association*

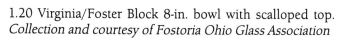

1.21 Left, Virginia/Foster Block two-handled covered bowl, D. 7 1/4 in.; right, finger bowl with scalloped top on scalloped saucer, D. 5 3/8 in. *Collection and courtesy of Fostoria Ohio Glass Association*

1.22 Virginia/Foster Block and other table accessories, such as syrups and shakers, were fitted with metal tops which were made by other companies; left, syrup, H. 7 in.; center shaker H. 3 in.; right, syrup, H. 5 in. *Collection and Courtesy of Fostoria Ohio Glass Association*

1.23 Virginia/Foster Block 6 1/2-in. rose bowl, circa 1888. *Collection and courtesy of Fostoria Ohio Glass Association*

1.24 Virginia/Foster Block 5 1/2-in. comport (compote) with wine. *Collection and courtesy of Fostoria Ohio Glass Association*

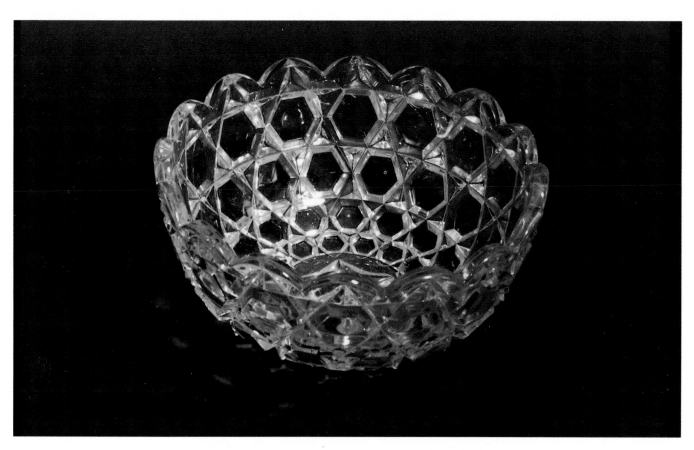

1.25 Virginia/Foster Block 9-in. bowl with scalloped top.
Collection and courtesy of Fostoria Ohio Glass Association

1.26 Virginia/Foster Block footed compote with scalloped top,
H. 7 1/4 in., D. 7 1/2 in. *Collection and courtesy of Fostoria
Ohio Glass Association*

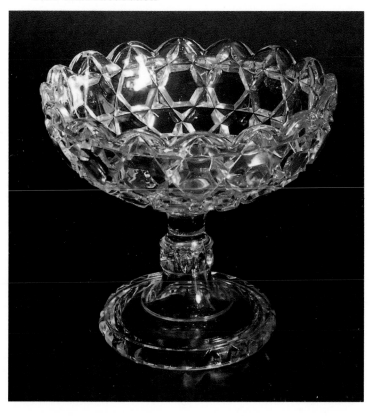

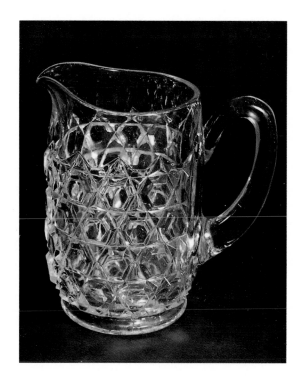

1.27 Virginia/Foster Block pitcher circa 1888, H. 8 in.
Collection and courtesy of Fostoria Ohio Glass Association

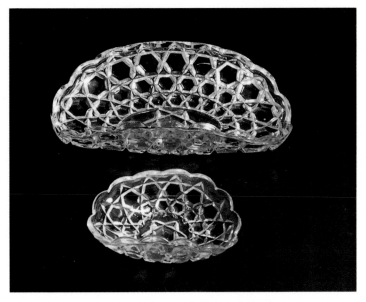

1.28 Virginia/Foster Block folded bowls, top, L. 9 3/4 in.; bottom L. 5 1/2 in. *Collection and courtesy of Fostoria Ohio Glass Association*

1.30 Yellow Virginia/Foster Block; left, goblet, H. 5 3/4 in.; center, wine, H. 4 1/2 in.; right tumbler, H. 3 3/4 in. *Collection and courtesy of Fostoria Ohio Glass Association*

1.29 Virginia/Foster Block 2-in. salts and round inkwell, D. 3 1/8 in. *Collection and courtesy of Fostoria Ohio Glass Association*

1.31 Captain Kidd was the name given to this pattern after another company pirated the Virginia/Foster Block pattern and Fostoria reintroduced it; left, red goblet, H. 5 3/4 in.; center, red handled mug, H. 3 1/4 in.; right, red sugar, W. 6 1/2 in. *Collection and courtesy of Fostoria Ohio Glass Association*

1.32 Red Captain Kidd two-handled jar, similar to sugar but narrower, H. 4 1/2 in.; right, juice tumbler, H. 3 3/4 in. *Collection and courtesy of Fostoria Ohio Glass Association*

1.33 Pressed pattern No. 141 Sterling, with ruffled tops and engraved leaf decoration, was introduced in 1888 with Foster Block and appeared together in an advertisement on the cover of the Dec. 27, 1888 issue of *Pottery and Glassware Reporter*, left, deep footed bowl, H. 4 3/4 in.; top center, footed vase, H. 6 1/2 in.; bottom center, shallow footed bowl, D. 4 1/2 in.; right, short footed vase, H. 4 1/2 in. *Collection and courtesy of Fostoria Ohio Glass Association*

1.34 Pressed pattern No. 162 Late Icicle was introduced about 1889; 3-pint jug, H. 9 in. *Collection and courtesy of Fostoria Ohio Glass Association*

162 3-pint Jug.
Packed 2 doz. in bbl

1.35 Late Icicle 3-pint jug illustrated in 1901 cagalog.

1.36 Left, Late Icicle small (cream) pitcher, H. 5 in.; center, covered (sugar) jar, H. 7 3/4 in.; right, footed spooner , H. 4 3/4 in. *Collection and courtesy of Fostoria Ohio Glass Associaton*

1.37 Left, Late Icicle cruet, H. 5 1/2 in.; center, jar fitted with metal base, lid and handle, H. 9 1/2 in.; right, goblet, H. 5 3/ 4 in. *Collection and courtesy of Fostoria Ohio Glass Association*

1.38 Late Icicle covered handled bowl, D. 7 in. *Collection and courtesy of Fostoria Ohio Glass Association*

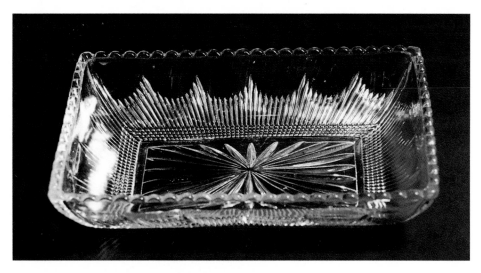

1.39 Late Icicle relish dish or baker. *Collection and courtesy of Fostoria Ohio Glass Association*

1.40 Pressed pattern No. 175 Fostoria Swirl was introduced in crystal and frosted crystal about 1890; left, frosted covered sugar, H. 5 1/2 in., D. 7 in.; center, frosted individual cream, H. 3 in.; right, frosted cream pitcher, H. 5 in. *Collection and courtesy of Fostoria Ohio Glass Association*

1.41 Left, Fostoria Swirl frosted spoon, H. 4 in.; center, clear spoon or celery, H. 6 in.; right, clear cruet, H. 6 1/2 in. *Collection and courtesy of Fostoria Ohio Glass Association*

1.42 Fostoria Swirl frosted lemon bowl with cover, D. 6 1/2 in. *Collection and courtesy of Fostoria Ohio Glass Association*

1.43 Top, clear Fostoria Swirl oblong dish, L. 11 1/2 in.; bottom, frosted nappy, D. 4 1/2 in. *Collection and courtesy of Fostoria Ohio Glass Association*

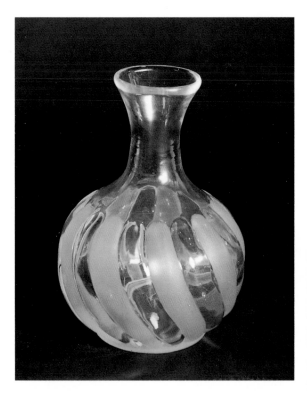

1.45 Pressed pattern No. 183 Victoria also came in both crystal and frosted. The heavy spiral and bull's-eye design was copied from a Baccarat pattern in 1890, patented by Fostoria's Lucien B. Martin, and appeared in an advertisement in the June 26, 1890 issue of *Pottery and Glassware Reporter*. The word 'Patented' in reverse appears on the outside base of some items, to be read from the other side. (Kamm 616) Left, 4-in. frosted rose bowl; center, 9-in. frosted serving bowl; right, individual frosted bowl, D. 4 3/4 in. *Collection and courtesy of Fostoria Ohio Glass Association*

1.44 Fostoria Swirl frosted decanter, H. 9 in. *Collection and courtesy of Fostoria Ohio Glass Association*

1.46 Left, frosted Victoria cream, H. 4 3/4 in.; center, frosted sugar, W. 7 1/2 in.; right, frosted spoon or celery, H. 5 3/4 in. *Collection and courtesy of Fostoria Ohio Glass Association*

1.47 Left, frosted Victoria syrup, H. 4 1/2 in.; center, frosted 3-cornered nappy, L. 6 1/2 in.; right, small spoon, H. 4 in. *Collection and courtesy of Fostoria Ohio Glass Association*

1.48 Left, frosted Victoria banana split, L. 7 3/4 in.; center, bowl, D. 8 1/4 in.; right, nappy, D. 5 1/4 in. *Collection and courtesy of Fostoria Ohio Glass Association*

1.49 Frosted Victoria covered butter, D. 7 in. *Collection and courtesy of Fostoria Ohio Glass Association*

1.51 Frosted Victoria pitcher, H. 7 3/4 in. *Collection and courtesy of Fostoria Ohio Glass Association*

1.50 Left, frosted Victoria shaker, H. 3 1/3 in.; center, frosted cup and saucer, D. 4 3/4 in.; right, frosted toothpick, H. 2 3/8 in. *Collection and courtesy of Fostoria Ohio Glass Association*

1.52 Victoria crystal jar fitted with metal base, lid, and handle with tongs for sugar cubes, H. 11 in. *Collection and courtesy of Fostoria Ohio Glass Association*

1.53 Victoria crystal decanter, H. 8 1/4 in. *Collection and courtesy of Fostoria Ohio Glass Association*

1.55 Left, Victoria shaker, H. 3 in.; top center, 6 1/2-in. rose bowl; bottom center, toothpick, H. 2 1/4 in.; right, 4 1/2-in. rose bowl. *Collection and courtesy of Fostoria Ohio Glass Association*

1.54 Left, Victoria cream or syrup, H. 4 in.; center, covered butter, D. 7 in.; right, cruet, H. 6 1/2 in. *Collection and courtesy of Fostoria Ohio Glass Association*

1.56 Top, Victoria centerpiece bowl, D. 10 1/2 in.; bottom, banana split, L. 8 in. *Collection and courtesy of Fostoria Ohio Glass Association*

1.57 Left, Victoria spoon, H. 4 in.; center, jar mounted with metal cover and handle, H. 11 in.; right, juice tumbler, H. 3 7/8 in. *Collection and courtesy of Fostoria Ohio Glass Association*

1.58 Some patterns were given numbers but not names; these pressed vases No. 184 were introduced about 1891; left, clear crystal, H. 11 in.; right, frosted with clear, H. 9 3/4 in. *Collection and courtesy of Fostoria Ohio Glass Association*

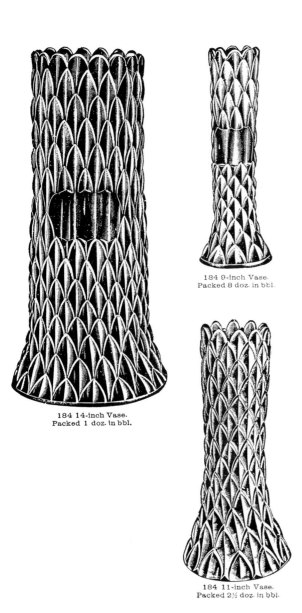

184 14-inch Vase.
Packed 1 doz. in bbl.

184 9-inch Vase.
Packed 8 doz. in bbl.

184 11-inch Vase.
Packed 2½ doz. in bbl.

1.59 No. 184 vases illustrated in 1901 catalog.

1.60 Pressed vases No. 195 introduced about 1891; left, frosted and clear, H. 5 in.; right, clear, H. 8 1/2 in. *Collection and courtesy of Fostoria Ohio Glass Association*

1.61 Pressed No. 200 Verona with needle etched band; left, spoon, H. 4 1/8 in.; center, spoon or celery, H. 6 1/2 in. right, cream, H. 5 in. *Collection and courtesy of Fostoria Ohio Glass Association*

1.62 Left, Verona sugar, D. 6 1/2 in. ; right, covered butter, D. 7 1/8 in. *Collection and courtesy of Fostoria Ohio Glass Association*

1.63 This 9-in. bowl is in the pressed pattern No. 205 Artichoke, introduced in 1891 in both clear crystal and etched, which is called Frosted Artichoke. The pattern was advertised in the Oct. 7, 1891 issue of *China Glass & Lamps. Collection and courtesy of Fostoria Ohio Glass Association*

1.65 Frosted Artichoke footed compote with cover, H. 11 in. *Collection and courtesy of Fostoria Ohio Glass Association*

1.64 Left, Frosted Artichoke nappy, D. 5 1/4 in.; center, 3-cornered nappy, L. 6 in.; right, nappy with plain rim, D. 4 5/8 in. *Collection and courtesy of Fostoria Ohio Glass Association*

1.66 Left, Frosted Artichoke finger bowl and plate, D. 6 1/8 in.; center, footed compote, H. 7 1/2 in., D. 9 1/4 in.; right, covered compote, D. 6 1/4 in. *Collection and courtesy of Fostoria Ohio Glass Association*

1.67 Left, Frosted Artichoke syrup with metal cover, H. 8 in.; right, pitcher, H. 9 3/4 in. *Collection and courtesy of Fostoria Ohio Glass Association*

1.68 Left, Frosted Artichoke sugar, H. 7 in.; top center, footed cake tray, D. 10 1/2 in.; bottom center, spoon or juice tumbler, H. 4 in.; right, cruet, H. 6 1/4 in. *Collection and courtesy of Fostoria Ohio Glass Association*

1.69 Pressed pattern No. 234 Rococo introduced in 1891; bowl with four short nubby vertically ribbed feet and two handles, L. 10 in. *Collection and courtesy of Fostoria Ohio Glass Association*

1.70 Rococo also came in a partly frosted version, as this 3-sided bowl with four feet, W. 6 in. *Collection and courtesy of Fostoria Ohio Glass Association*

1.71 Pressed pattern No. 272 introduced in the early 1890s and illustrated in the May 2, 1894 issue of *China, Glass, & Lamps*, tapered footed vase, H. 8 in. *Collection and courtesy of Fostoria Ohio Glass Association*

Vases.

1.72 Vase No. 272 illustrated in the 1901 catalog.

272 14-inch Vase.
Packed 2 doz. in bbl.

272 11½-inch Vase.
Packed 3 doz. in bbl.

272 8-inch Vase.
Packed 10 doz. in bbl.

272 5½-inch Vase.
Packed 15 doz. in bbl.

1.73 Pressed pattern Diamond Mirror, without a number, but introduced around 1890; left, small footed ice bucket or vase, H. 5 in.; center, toothpick, H. 2 1/4 in.; right, footed ice bucket or vase, H. 6 in. *Collection and courtesy of Fostoria Ohio Glass Association*

1.74 Left, Diamond Mirror goblet, H. 6 in.; center, jar with metal cover, H. 6 1/2 in.; right, small footed compote or sherbet, H. 4 3/4 in. *Collection and courtesy of Fostoria Ohio Glass Association*

1.75 Left, Diamond Mirror nappy, D. 4 3/4 in.; top center, footed centerpiece bowl, D. 10 in.; bottom center, salt, D. 3 in.; right, footed bowl, D. 7 1/4 in. *Collection and courtesy of Fostoria Ohio Glass Association*

1.76 Diamond Mirror footed compote with cover, H. 13 in. *Collection and courtesy of Fostoria Ohio Glass Association*

1.77 Diamond Mirror pitcher, H. 7 3/4 in. *Collection and courtesy of Fostoria Ohio Glass Association*

1.78 Pressed pattern No. 301 Lorraine, the last number of pressed ware to be made in Fostoria, Ohio; left, decanter with stopper, H. 6 1/2 in.; right, shaker with metal top, H. 3 1/4 in. *Collection and courtesy of Fostoria Ohio Glass Association*

1.79 These Annie Rooney night lamps were intentionally made with mixed patterns of Frosted Artichoke shades with Foster Block bases and were illustrated in the July 3, 1890 issue of *Crockery and Glass Journal. Collection and courtesy of Fostoria Ohio Glass Association*

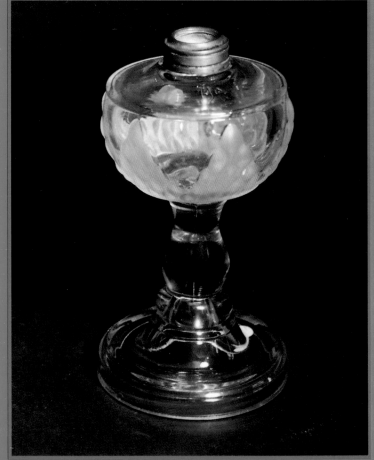

1.80 Frosted Artichoke stand lamp, H. 8 in., illustrated in the June 24, 1891 issue of *China, Glass, & Lamps. Collection and courtesy of Fostoria Ohio Glass Association*

1.81 Late Icicle (Icicle) stand lamp, H. 9 1/2 in., illustrated in the July 18, 1889 issue of *Pottery and Glassware Reporter*. *Collection and courtesy of Fostoria Ohio Glass Association*

1.82 Artichoke stand lamp, H. 20 in. including chimney, advertised in the June 24, 1891 issue of *China, Glass, & Lamps*. *Collection and courtesy of Fostoria Ohio Glass Association*

1.83 Frosted Artichoke stand lamp, H. 16 14 in. including chimney, advertised in the June 24, 1891 issue of *China, Glass, & Lamps. Collection and courtesy of Fostoria Ohio Glass Association*

1.84 Rare Frosted Artichoke foot hand lamp with handle, H. 13 in., illustrated in the June 24, 1891 issue of *China, Glass, & Lamps. Collection and courtesy of Fostoria Ohio Glass Association*

1.85 Virginia/Foster Block stand lamp with metal base and opaque white shade over the chimney. *Collection and courtesy of Fostoria Ohio Glass Association*

1.86 The pattern on the font of this banquet lamp resembles railroad signals, but the pattern is not known or named; H. 32 in. to top of shade, circa 1888, signed on thumbwheel FOSTORIA GLASS CO. FOSTORIA OHIO. *Collection and courtesy of Fostoria Ohio Glass Association*

1.87 Cascade banquet lamp, H. 32 1/2 in. to top of shade, signed on thumbwheel FOSTORIA GLASS CO. FOSTORIA OHIO. *Collection and courtesy of Fostoria Ohio Glass Association*

1.88 Cascade banquet candelabra with U drop prisms, center H. 27 1/2 in. (without candles) illustrated in Dec. 26, 1889 issue of *Pottery and Glassware Reporter. Collection and courtesy of Fostoria Ohio Glass Association*

1.89 Victoria banquet lamp with metal pedestal and glass font, H. 22 1/2 in. including chimney. *Collection and courtesy of Fostoria Ohio Glass Association*

Chapter 2

American

Designed by Phillip Ebeling and patented in 1915, the American pattern line No. 2056 was Fostoria's best seller for over 70 years. The original issue of 95 items was made only in crystal. During the 1920s, when color was introduced to other Fostoria patterns, both pastels and some deeper colors were used for the American line. Ruby and milk glass were added later and are far more common today than the early pastels.

In addition to enjoying coast-to-coast domestic popularity, barrels of American pattern were shipped to England, particularly pitcher sets and wash bowls in the 1920s and 1930s. Table settings remained the United States staple; they were attractive, moderately priced, and utilitarian. The enormous success led to an expanded line of 340 pieces plus colors and experimental or one-of-a-kind items. According to Kenneth Dalzell, "a workman often played with a piece, and when he left at the end of the day it went out with his lunch bucket." Atypical American colors may also turn up. If a batch was prepared for a particular pattern, it was not uncommon for a worker to pick up any mold (which may well have been American) to test some pieces.

Most items were standard and cataloged, so it is possible to determine the time frame during which they were produced. If the production time was short, a fairly accurate date can be attributed to the piece. However, many items were made continuously, using the same molds, for 70 years. According to Sidney Seligson, the older pieces can often be distinguished by rounder cube edges and a more brilliant color due to fire polishing. (Seligson 5)

After Fostoria closed in 1986, the new owners, Lancaster Colony, received the original molds.

Dalzell-Viking of New Martinsville, West Virginia, has been contracted to produce items of the American pattern, as well as some other Fostoria favorites, from these molds. The new Fostoria and new Viking glass is called "American crystal" (in contrast to European crystal) and has a brighter, clearer look than earlier glass. In the past, a soda-lime content gave glass a greenish or yellowish cast unless decolorizers such as powder blue and manganese were added to counteract the lime. Lead was another ingredient in some of the original Fostoria, and today lead has been replaced by barium and zinc. In addition to subtle color differences, the American being made today is a bit denser and heavier. Shapes may also vary slightly, according to Dalzell. These color, weight, and shape variations are best detected when two like pieces, one old and one new, are compared side by side.

Since the American pattern was pressed, mold marks are visible on the glass unless the mold was in one piece and the glass was "dumped out," as in the case of the banana split. (Seligson 2) American Whitehall is a later variant of American and is made by another Lancaster Colony company, the Indiana Glass Co. of Dunkirk, Indiana. Whitehall often has more pronounced mold marks as well as thicker and blunter edges. Some shapes are a bit different, such as a punch cup with the addition of a short stem between the bowl and the foot. Other shapes, like the covered votive candle which resembles a rose bowl cut through the middle, were not used for original American. Colors are also different from American.

When one considers that hundreds of individual items plus colors were turned out between 1915 and 1986, and some are being produced today, this single pattern offers many

challenges to the collector. Where did all of this glass go? As with any breakable, much has been lost, yet thousands of pieces remain in use, in cupboards, and in collections. Whether a collector is assembling a usable service or seeks the rare and unusual, this classic pattern can accommodate both.

2.1 **Top row**: No. 2, 10-oz. goblet with hex foot, H. 6 7/8 in; No. 3, 9-oz. low goblet, H. 5 1/2 in.; No. 25, 7-oz. claret, H. 4 7/8 in; No. 26, 2 1/2-oz. wine, H. 4 3/8 in.; No. 63, 12-oz. luncheon goblet/ice tea, H. 5 3/4 in.; No. 88, 5-oz. footed tumbler, H. 4 3/4 in.

Center row: No. 10, 4 1/2-oz. regular high sherbet, H. 4 1/2 in.; No. 9, 4 1/2-oz. flared high sherbet, H. 4 3/8 in.; No. 5, 4 1/2-oz. footed dessert with hex foot, H. 4 3/8 in.; No. 12, 5-oz. flared low sherbet, H. 3 1/4 in.; No. 13, 5-oz. regular low sherbet, H. 3 1/2 in.; No 16, 6-oz. sundae, H. 3 1/8 in.

Bottom row: No. 64, 12-oz. regular ice tea, H. 5 in.; No. 65, 12-oz. flared ice tea, H. 5 1/4 in.; No. 89, 5-oz. regular tumbler, H. 3 5/8 in.; No. 76, 8-oz. table tumbler, H. 3 7/8 in.; No. 709, 12-oz. tankard, H. 4 1/2 in. *Catalog photo courtesy of Lancaster Colony*

American Stemware

Goblet — Low Goblet — Claret — Wine — Luncheon Goblet/ Ice Tea — Footed Tumbler

High Sherbet Regular — High Sherbet Flared — Footed Dessert — Low Sherbet Flared — Low Sherbet Regular — Sundae

Ice Tea Regular — Ice Tea Flared — Tumbler Regular — Table Tumbler — Tankard — York Double Old Fashioned — York High Ball

2.2a **Top row**: No. 620, 2-part relish, L. 12 in.; No. 211, 10-in. salad bowl; No. 286, 4-piece salad set; No. 567, 14-in. torte plate; No. 987, salad utensils; No 241, 11 3/4-in. oval bowl.
Bottom row: No. 129, 12-in large boat; No. 300, oblong butter and cover, L. 7 1/2 in.; No. 128, 8 1/2-in. small boat; No. 306, 10-in. handled cake plate.

2.2b **Top row**: No. 448, jelly, H. 4 1/2 in.; No. 347, footed candy with cover, H. 7 in.; No. 47, bell; No. 386, 5-in. compote and cover, H. 9 in.; No. 447, jelly and cover, H. 6 3/4 in.; No. 762, 6-in. footed bud vase, cupped; No. 798, 8 1/2-in. footed bud vase, cupped; No. 763, 6-in. footed bud vase, flared; No. 799, 8 1/2-in. footed bud vase, flared.
Bottom row: No. 222, 10 1/2-in. 3-toed bowl; No. 505, 5-in. nappy and cover, H. 5 in.; No. 363, 11-in. 3-cornered centerpiece. *Catalog photo courtesy of Lancaster Colony*

American Giftware

American Giftware

2.3a **Top row**: No. 554, 10 1/2-in. sandwich plate; No. 552, 9 1/2-in. dinner plate; No. 550, 8 1/2-in. salad plate; No. 549, 7-in. salad plate; No. 661, 6 1/2-oz. cheese/sugar shaker, H. 5 1/4-in.; No. 704, 6 1/2-oz. dripcut syrup, H. 5 1/4 in.
Center row: No. 360, 10-in. celery; No. 649, shaker and chrome top A, H. 3 1/2 in.; No. 650, individual shaker and chrome top C, H. 2 3/8 in.; No. 495, 4 1/2-in. nappy, No. 502, 4 1/2-in. handled square nappy; No. 499, 4 1/2-in. handled regular nappy; No. 501, 5-in. 3-cornered handled nappy.
Bottom row: No. 540, 8-in. pickle; No. 536, 6-in. olive; No. 421, 4 3/4-in. nappy/fruit; No. 492, napkin ring, D. 2-in.; No. 307, 12-in. footed cake plate.

2.3b **Top row**: No. 521, 8-in. nappy; No. 517, 7-in. nappy; No. 866 picture frame; No. 548, 6-in. bread and butter; No. 314, 3-in. candlestick; No.331, twin candlesticks, H. 4 3/4 in.; No. 319, 6-in. candlestick.
Center row: No. 512, 6-in. nappy; No. 506, 5-in. nappy; No. 732, 9-in. handled utility tray; No. 584, party server with 2 spoons; No. 632, individual salt, H. 1 in.; No. 673, handled sugar and cover, H. 5 1/4 in.; No. 674, handled sugar, H. 3 1/4 in.; No. 680, cream, H. 4 1/4 in.
Bottom row: No. 648, 9-in. handled serving dish; No. 396, footed cup; No. 397, saucer; No. 311, chamber candleholder, H. 2 in.; No. 836, 9-in. oval vegetable dish. *Catalog photo courtesy of Lancaster Colony*

2.4a **Top row**: No. 631, square salver, H. 7 1/4 in., 10-in. square; No.639, cake stand, H. 3 7/8 in., D. 10 1/2 in.; No. 630, round salver, H. 7 1/4 in.; D. 10 in.
Bottom row: No. 622, 3-part combination relish, L. 11 1/2 in.; No. 686, 3-piece individual sugar and cream with tray; No. 687, individual sugar, H. 2 3/8 in.; No. 688, 4-oz. individual cream, H. 3 in.; No. 697, 6 3/4 in. sugar and cream tray; No. 567, 14 in. torte plate.

2.4b **Top row**: No. 456, 3-pint ice jug, H. 6 1/2 in.; No. 458, 1/2-gal. lipped ice jug, H. 8 1/4 in.; No. 979, plastic punch ladle; No. 600, 14-in. 2-gal. punch bowl, H. 6 1/2 in.; No. 602, low foot for 14-in. punch bowl, H. 6 1/2 in.; No. 388, 5-in. compote, H. 6 1/4 in.
Bottom row: No. 707, 8 in. 3-toed tidbit; No. 137, 7 in. 3-toed bon bon; No. 614, footed punch cup; No. 377, coaster, D. 3 3/4 in. *Catalog photo courtesy of Lancaster Colony*

2.5 American Pattern. *Catalog photo courtesy of Lancaster Colony*

2.6 Detail of American pattern ice cube.

2.7 Left, No. 552, 9 1/2-in. dinner plate, 1936-82; right, No. 553 frosted 9-in. salad plate, 1915-71. *Collection of Joanne Parker*

2.8 Detail of sandwich plate.

2.9 Top, No. 549, 7-in salad plate, 1932-82; bottom, No. 540 pickle dish, L. 8 in., 1915-82. *Collection of Joanne Parker*

2.10 Top, No. 2056 1/2-622, combination 3-part relish, L. 11 in., W. 7 1/2 in., 1939-82; bottom, 3-part relish, L. 9 1/2 in., W. 6 in., 1935-44. *Courtesy of Second Hand Rose Antiques*

2.11 Top, crescent salad plate, L. 7 1/2 in., 1937-44; bottom, unusual small plate. *Collection of Joanne Parker*

2.12 No. 723, handled lunch tray, D. 12 in., 1940-74. *Courtesy of Second Hand Rose Antiques*

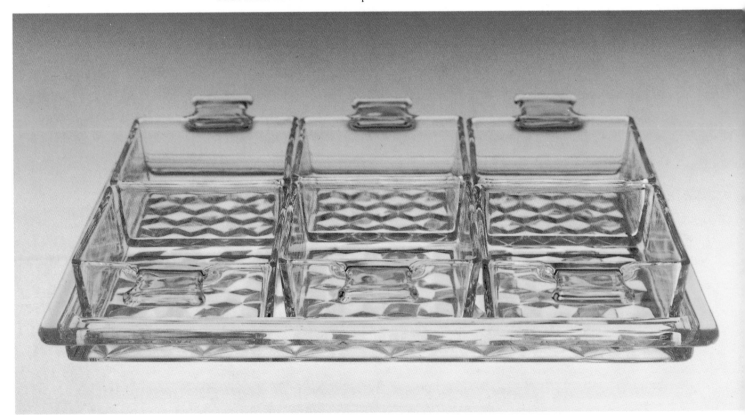

2.13 Ice cream or appetizer set with 10 1/2-in. oblong tray and six individual appetizers. *Collection of Joanne Parker*

2.14 No. 631, 10-in. square cake salver, H. 7 1/4 in., 1924-42.
Collection of Joanne Parker

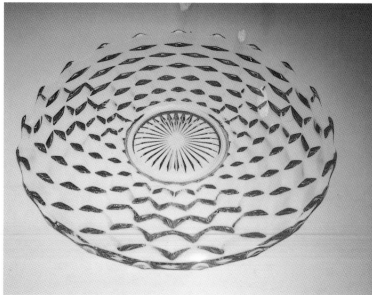

2.15 No. 307, 12-in. footed cake plate, 1939-83. *Collection of Rae Hamilton*

2.16 No. 567, 14-in. torte plate, 1933-1982. *Collection of Rae Hamilton*

2.17 No. 259, shrimp and attached sauce bowl, D. 12 1/4 in., 1959-74. *Collection of Joanne Parker*

2.18 No. 188, two-handled bowl, W. 8 1/2 in., H. 3 3/4 in., 1924-72. *Collection of Joanne Parker*

2.19 No. 600, 2-gal. 14-in. punch bowl, H. 6 1/2 in., 1915-82. *Courtesy of Second Hand Rose Antiques*

2.20 Basket with reed handle, H. 4 in., L. 9 in., 1940-58. *Courtesy of Second Hand Rose Antiques*

2.21 Ruffled bowl, probably the result of a glassmaker's experimentation and, therefore, unique, H. 3 1/2 in., D. 6 in. *Collection of Joanne Parker*

2.22 Left, No. 478, mayonnaise (available with underplate and ladle), H. 3 3/8 in., D. 5 1/4 in., 1948-74; right, 3 1/2-in. rose bowl, 1934-58. *Courtesy of Second Hand Rose Antiques*

2.23 Left, No. 505, 5-in. nappy with cover (same cover as footed candy), 1924-82; right, ice dish (uses tomato juice liner), D. 5 in., 1940-58. *Courtesy of Second Hand Rose Antiques*

2.24 No. 687, individual sugar, H. 2 1/2 in., 1916-82; right, No. 688, 4-oz. individual cream, H. 3 in., 1916-82, (also available with tray No. 697, the same tray used for tea sugar and cream). *Courtesy of Second Hand Rose Antiques*

2.26 Condiment set with 6 pieces, consisting of two 5-oz. oil bottles with stoppers, two shakers, mustard with cover and spoon, and 10 1/2-in. cloverleaf shaped tray, which will not hold the larger 7-oz. cruets, 1924-44. *Collection of Joanne Parker*

2.25 Left, early necked rose bowl with metal lid and spoon, H. 5 1/2 in. including lid; right, sugar or cheese shaker with tall metal top, H. without top 4 3/4 in., H. with top 6 1/2 in. *Collection of Joanne Parker*

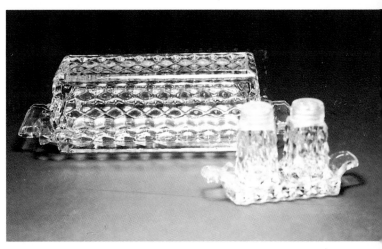

2.27 Left, 4 1/2-oz. handled sherbet, H. 3 1/2 in., 1916-44; center, covered straw jar, H. 12 in., D. 4 in., 1915-28; right, No. 2056 1/2-441, jam pot set with covered jam pots, H. 4 1/2 in., 1948-71, and sugar and cream tray, L. 6 3/4 in., W. 4 in., 1939-74. *Collection of Joanne Parker*

2.29 Left, No. 2056 1/2-300, covered oblong butter, L 7 1/2 in., W. 3 1/4 in., 1940-82; right, No. 662, 3-piece individual shaker set, shaker with glass top, H. 2 1/4 in. (also available with chrome tops), tray L. 4 in., 1924-82. *Collection of Joanne Parker*

2.30 Left, small ice tub, H. 3 3/4 in., D. 5 5/8 in., 1915-58; right, larger ice tub, H. 4 1/2 in., D. 6 1/2 in., 1916-60, (also available with underplates which are different from the salad or dinner plates). *Collection of Joanne Parker*

2.28 No. 297, round covered butter, 1915-74. *Collection of Joanne Parker*

2.31 Left, No. 454, 1-qt. jug or boudoir pitcher, H. 7 1/4 in., 1915-74; right, No. 455, 3-pt. jug or boudoir pitcher, H. 8 in., 1915-74. *Collection of Joanne Parker*

2.32 Left, No. 88, 5-oz. footed tumbler, H. 4 3/4 in, 1934-82; top center, No. 3, 9-oz. low goblet, H. 5 1/2 in., 1932-82; bottom center, No. 100, 2-oz. whiskey, H. 2 1/2 in., 1934-75; right, No. 33, 4 1/2-oz. oyster cocktail, H. 3 1/2 in. *Courtesy of Second Hand Rose Antiques*

2.33 Left, No. 12, 5-oz. low flared sherbet, H. 3 1/4 in., 1924-82; right, No. 448, jelly, (also available with cover), H. 4 1/4 in., D. 4 1/4 in., 1916-82. *Courtesy of Second Hand Rose Antiques*

2.34 Left, No. 9, 4 1/2-oz. high flared sherbet, H. 4 3/8 in., 1924-82; right, No. 388, 5-in. comport (also available with cover), H. 6 1/4 in., 1924-82. *Courtesy of Second Hand Rose Antiques*

2.35 Left, flared punch cup with flat handle, made until 1971; center, small footed whiskey; right, No. 21, cone footed 3-oz. cocktail, H. 2 7/8 in., 1935-70. *Courtesy of Second Hand Rose Antiques*

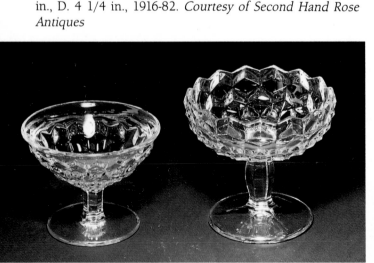

2.36 Water bottle with wood stopper, 44-oz capacity, H. 9 1/4 in.
without stopper, 1916-27. *Collection of Joanne Parker*

2.37 Crushed fruit jar with cover made to accommodate crushed fruit spoon; the lids were made in limited production and were often damaged by the spoons, making the lids a rare item today; the bottom is the same as for the cookie jar. H. 10 in., D. 5 3/4 in., 1915-28. *Collection of Joanne Parker*

2.39 No. 400, decanter set with 24-oz. decanters with ground necks and ground stoppers, etched labels Scotch and Rye, H. 9 1/4 in., 1933-66. *Collection of Joanne Parker*

2.38 Cookie, cracker, or pretzel jar with cover (same bottom as for crushed fruit and humidor), H. 8 3/4 in., D. 5 3/4 in., 1915-44, but a new version, No. 362 is pictured in the 1961 catalog. *Collection of Joanne Parker*

2.40 Plain 24-oz. decanters in early rack with caps and central handle. *Collection of Joanne Parker*

2.41 Left, banana split boat. L. 9 in., W. 3 1/2 in., 1915-28; right, tobacco humidor with rounded dull bronze top (the bottom is the same as the crushed fruit and cookie jar), H. 4 3/4 in. without top. *Collection of Joanne Parker*

2.42 Left, large 8-oz. cologne, H. 7 1/4 in., 1925-44; center, oblong tray, L. 5 in., W. 2 1/2 in., 1917-44; right, sugar cuber with bottom resembling round puff, and metal cover with spring loaded sugar tongs on top, H. 2 7/8 in., 1916-28. *Collection of Joanne Parker*

2.43 Left, flared baby tumbler, 1957-60; center, covered 12-oz. pickle jar, H. 6 in., 1915-28; right, 4 1/2-oz. bitters bottle with tube, H. 5 3/4 in, 1934-43. *Collection of Joanne Parker*

2.44 Small 6-oz. cologne, H. 5 3/4 in., and puff boxes fitted into brass filigree holders with floral medalions; these brass frames were made by other companies, often in Europe. *Collection of Joanne Parker*

2.45 Rare 10-in. bagged vase with high shoulder and flared mouth, 1924-27. *Collection of Joanne Parker*

2.46 Left, pickle or jam jar fitted with metal top, H. 4 1/2 in., 1915-28; right, 10-in. cupped vase, 1924-43. *Collection of Joanne Parker*

2.47 Lamp made from 12-in. straight vase, fitted with metal base and cap. *Collection of Joanne Parker*

2.48 Straight vases: top left, 10-in. vase, 1915-1958; bottom left, No. 785, 8-in. vase, 1915-1970; top right, 12-in vase, 1915-44; bottom right, No. 757, 6-in. vase, 1933-70. *Collection of Joanne Parker*

2.50 Flared square vase (similar to 7 1/2-in.high urn with foot), H. 7 1/2 in. *Courtesy of Second Hand Rose Antiques*

2.49 Flared vases: left, No. 2056 1/2-786, 8-in. vase, 1935-74; center, No. 2056 1/2-758, 6-in. vase, 1935-74; right, No. 2056 1/2-815, 10-in. vase, 1939-70. *Collection of Joanne Parker*

2.51 Unusual bud vase stretched from footed tumbler, probably an experimental piece, H. 8 in. *Collection of Joanne Parker*

2.52 Left, cigarette box with lid, L. 4 3/4 in., W. 3 1/2 in., 1935-58; top right, bell, 1981-82 (the short production time makes the bell a high demand item even though it is of recent issue); bottom right, small oval tray. *Collection of Joanne Parker*

2.55 Topper ashtray, D. 2 1/8 in. 1934-58. *Courtesy of Second Hand Rose Antiques*

2.53 Left, flared baby bowl, 1958-60, D. 4 1/4 in.; right napkin ring, D. 2 in., 1974-82. *Courtesy of Jerry Gallagher*

2.56 Pink 3-in topper, D. 4 1/2 in., original crystal issue 1940-58; this is a more recent example. *Collection of Joanne Parker*

2.54 No. 314, 3-in. candlesticks, 1937-82. *Courtesy of Second Hand Rose Antiques*

2.57 Top left, individual sugar, H. 2 1/2 in., in amber, introduced in 1925; bottom left, regular nappy in green, mid-1920s; right, individual cream, H. 2 3/4 in., in rose, introduced 1928. *Collection of Joanne Parker*

2.58 Sugar and cream in green. *Photo courtesy of Jerry Gallagher*

2.59 Unusual orchid vase. *Collection of Joanne Parker*

2.60 Deep nappy in orchid, D. 8 in., H. 4 3/4 in., introduced in 1927. *Collection of Joanne Parker*

2.61 Smokey brown 12-oz. mugs, H. 4 1/2 in. *Collection of Joanne Parker*

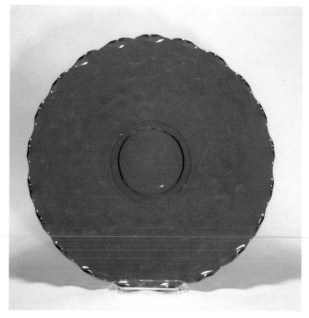

2.62 No. 567, 14-in. torte plate in ruby, being made today. *Collection of Joanne Parker*

2.63 Left, No. 763, flared hexagonal footed 6-in. bud vase in ruby; center, No. 137, 3-toed bon bon in ruby, D. 7 in., H. 2 in.; right, No. 347, footed candy jar with cover in ruby, H. 7 in. *Collection of Joanne Parker*

2.65 American pattern milk glass was produced from 1953 to 1965; left, No. 162, wedding bowl with cover, H. 8 in.; right, No. 763, flared hexagonal footed 6-in. bud vase. *Collection of Joanne Parker*

2.64 Left, ruby candy jar with cover and hexagonal foot, H. 7 in.; right, blue 3-toed bonbon, D. 7 in. *Collection of Joanne Parker*

2.66 Left, No 763, flared hexagonal-footed 6-in. bud vase in aqua, produced 1957-59; center, No. 804, flared square footed 9-in. vase, 1953-65; right, 4-in. topper, 1953-59. *Collection of Joanne Parker*

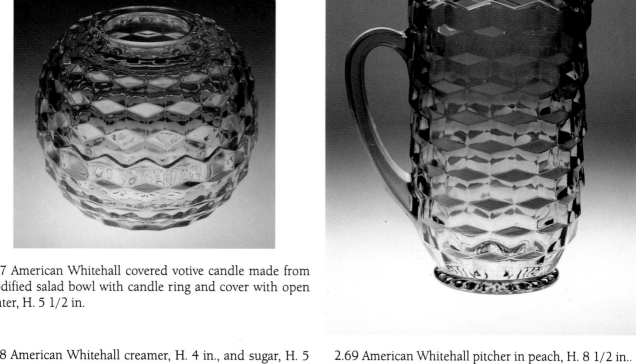

2.67 American Whitehall covered votive candle made from modified salad bowl with candle ring and cover with open center, H. 5 1/2 in.

2.68 American Whitehall creamer, H. 4 in., and sugar, H. 5 in., in peach. Creamer with paper label ITEM # 1979 AMERICAN WHITEHALL CREAMER, PEACH Indiana Glass Co. A Lancaster Colony Company, Dunkirk, Ind. 47336. Sugar # 1981 with same label.

2.69 American Whitehall pitcher in peach, H. 8 1/2 in..

2.70 Pattern No. 5056, American Lady blown lead glass stemware, 1934-72: left, No. 2, 10-oz. goblet, H. 6 1/8 in.; right, No. 11, 5 1/2-oz. sherbet, H. 4 1/8 in. *Collection of Joanne Parker*

2.71 Left, American Lady No. 21, 3 1/2-oz. cocktail, H. 4 1/8 in.; center, N. 63, 12-oz. luncheon goblet/ice tea, H. 5 1/2 in.; right, No. 88, 5-oz. footed tumbler, H. 4 1/8 in., 1934-72. *Collection of Joanne Parker*

2.72 Left, American Lady 10-oz goblet, H. 6 1/8 in.; right, 3 1/2-oz claret wine, H. 4 5/8 in., both in burgundy, 1933-1973. *Photo courtesy of Jerry Gallagher*

2.73 Left, footed 5-oz. tumbler in burgundy with crystal base, H. 4 1/8 in., 1934-1963; center, 1-oz. cordial in empire green with crystal base, H. 3 1/8 in., 1934-42; right, 5 1/2-oz. sherbet in crystal, H. 4 1/8 in., 1934-72. *Collection of Joanne Parker*

Chapter 3

Coin

Coin was originally a nineteenth-century pattern made by the Central Glass Co. of Wheeling, West Virginia. When Fostoria introduced it in 1958, the shapes were adapted from earlier Fostoria patterns: turn-of-the-century No. 1299 Long Buttress, No. 1372 Essex, and the No. 2222 Colonial pattern of the 1920s. These early designs were modified to make some of the Coin items, and new shapes were introduced for others. Coin No.1372 Line was made in five colors: ruby, amber, blue, olive green, and emerald green. There are four coins in the pattern: Liberty Bell, Colonial Man, Torch, and Eagle with the 1887 date, the year Fostoria was founded. From 1961 to 1983, Fostoria also made Coin for Avon with the date 1886, the year that Avon was founded. Some of the regular Coin, which was discontinued in 1982, is currently being produced by Dalzell-Viking for Lancaster Colony.

3.1a No. 1372/162, ruby, blue, and amber wedding bowls with cover, H. 8 1/4 in.

Coin Glass Giftware

Ruby COO5/162   Blue COO3/162   Amber COO2/162

3.1b Ruby Coin; **top row**: No. 316, 4 1/2-in. candleholder; No. 326, 8-in. candleholder; No. 799, 8-in. bud vase; No.199, 8 1/2-in. footed bowl; No. 673, sugar and cover, H. 5 3/4 in.; No. 680, cream, H. 3 1/2 in.
Center row: No. 354, candy box and cover, H. 4 1/8 in., D. 6 3/8 in.; No. 347, candy jar and cover, H. 6 3/4 in.; No. 179, 8-in. bowl.
Bottom row: No. 189, 9-in. oval bowl; No. 123, 5-in. ash tray; No. 119, 7 1/2-in. center coin ash tray. *Catalog photo courtesy of Lancaster Colony*

3.2 No. 737 condiment set consisting of No. 531, 7-oz. cruet in crystal, 1964-70; No. 652, pair of ruby shakers with chrome tops, H. 3 1/4 in.; No. 738, tray in crystal, L. 9 5/8 in. 1964-70. *Collection of Joanne Parker*

3.3 Left, No. 7, 9-oz. sherbet, H. 5 3/8 in., 1969-70; center, No. 2, tall goblet, H. 6 5/8 in., 1969-70; right, No. 26, 5-oz. wine, H. 5 3/16 in., 1969-70, all in ruby and also available in crystal and olive green. *Collection of Glenn and Betty Close*

3.4 Center, No. 179, 8-in. round bowl in ruby, 1967-82, (available in other colors 1960-82); No. 326 8-in. candlesticks in ruby, 1968-82, (other colors 1968-81). *Collection of Glenn and Betty Close*

3.5 Center, No. 189, 9-in. oval bowl in ruby, 1967-82, (other colors 1960-82); No. 316 4 1/2-in. candlesticks in ruby, 1967-82, (other colors 1960-82). *Collection of Glenn and Betty Close*

3.6 No. 199, 8 1/2-in. footed compote in ruby, 1967-82, (other colors 1961-82). *Collection of Glenn and Betty Close*

3.7 Left, No. 673, covered sugar in ruby, H. 5 3/8 in., 1973-82, (other colors 1960-82); center, No. 652, shakers in ruby with chrome tops, H. 3 1/2 in., 1973-78, (other colors 1964-78); right, No. 680, cream in ruby, H. 3 1/2 in., 1973-82, (other colors 1960-82). *Collection of Glenn and Betty Close*

3.8 No. 829, tall footed urn and cover in ruby, H. 12 3/4 in., 1967-81, (other colors 1962-81). *Collection of Glenn and Betty Close*

3.9 Left, No. 354, low covered candy box in ruby, H. 4 1/8 in., D. 6 3/8 in., 1967-82, (other colors 1960-82); center, No. 381, cigarette urn in ruby, H. 3 3/8 in., 1972-81, (other colors 1964-81); right, No. 499, handled nappy in ruby, D. 5 3/8 in., 1967-81, (other colors 1960-81). *Collection of Glenn and Betty Close*

3.10 No. 829, tall footed urn and cover in amber, H. 12 3/4 in., 1962-81. *Collection of Glenn and Betty Close*

3.11 Detail of amber torch coin.

3.12 Left, No. 673, amber covered sugar, H. 5 3/8 in., 1963-82; center, No. 162, amber wedding bowl and cover, H. 8 3/16 in., 1962-82, (other colors, 1958-82); right, No. 680, amber cream, H. 3 1/2 in., 1963-82. *Collection of Glenn and Betty Close*

3.13 Left, No. 354, amber low candy box and cover, H. 4 1/8 in., D. 6 3/8 in., 1961-82; bottom center, No. 381, amber cigarette urn, H. 3 3/8 in., 1964-81; top center, No. 799, amber 8-in. bud vase, 1961-82; right, No. 499, amber handled nappy, D. 5 3/8 in., 1961-81. *Collection of Glenn and Betty Close*

3.14 No. 199, amber 8 1/2-in. footed compote, 1961-82.
Collection of Glenn and Betty Close

3.15 Left, No. 453, amber 1-qt. pitcher, H. 6 9/16 in., 1963-
81; right, No. 179, amber 8-in. round bowl, 1961-82. *Collection
of Glenn and Betty Close*

3.16 Oil lamps, which also came in an electrified version, in amber with white striking on the globe pattern; left, No. 459, tall patio oil lamp in, H. 16 5/8 in., 1961-70, (crystal and blue 1961-66); right, No. 310, handled courting oil lamp in, H. 9 3/4 in., 1961-73, (blue 1961-66). *Collection of Glenn and Betty Close*

3.17 Left, No.162 wedding bowl and cover in ususual blue, H. 8 3/16 in., 1962-66 and 1975-82; right, same bowl in different blue. *Collection of Glenn and Betty Close*

3.18 Left, No. 354, blue low candy box and cover, H. 4 1/8 in., D. 6 3/8 in., 1961-66; center, No. 799, blue 8-in. bud vase, 1961-66 and 1975-82; right, No. 499, blue handled nappy, D. 5 3/8 in., 1961-66 and 1975-81. *Collection of Glenn and Betty Close*

3.19 Bottom, No. 652, blue shakers with chrome lids, H. 3 1/2 in., 1964-66 and 1975-78; top left, No. 680, blue cream, H. 3 1/2 in., 1963-66 and 1975-82; top right, No. 673, blue covered sugar, H. 5 3/8 in., 1963-66 and 1975-82. *Collection of Glenn and Betty Close*

3.20 Bottom, No. 652, olive green shakers with chrome lids, H. 3 1/2 in., 1964-78; top left, No. 347, olive green covered candy jar (taller than covered sugar) H. 6 3/4 in., 1965-81; top right, No. 680, olive green cream, H. 3 1/2 in., 1965-81. *Collection of Glenn and Betty Close*

3.21 Olive green No. 199, footed compote, D. 8 1/2 in., 1965-81. *Collection of Glenn and Betty Close*

3.22 Center, No. 189, olive green oval bowl, D. 9 in., 1965-81;
and No. 316, olive green 4 1/2-in. candlesticks, 1965-81.
Collection of Glenn and Betty Close

3.23 Center, No. 179, olive green round bowl, D. 8 in., 1965-
81; and No. 326, olive green 8-in. candlesticks, 1968-81.
Collection of Glenn and Betty Close

3.24 Left, No. 453, olive green 1-qt. pitcher, H. 6 9/16, 1965-81; bottom center, No. 448, olive green jelly or small footed compote, H. 3 3/4 in., 1965-81; top center, No. 162, olive green wedding bowl and cover, H. 8 3/16 in., 1963-80; right, No. 381, olive green cigarette urn, H. 3 3/8 in., 1965-81. *Collection of Glenn and Betty Close*

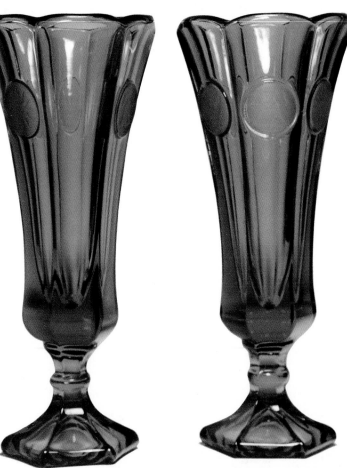

3.25 No. 799, olive green 8-in. bud vases, 1965-81. *Collection of Glenn and Betty Close*

3.26 Left, No. 114, 7 1/2-in. four coin ashtray in amber, 1960-81; right, in olive green, 1965-81. *Collection of Glenn and Betty Close*

3.27 Left, No. 114, 7 1/2-in. four coin ashtray in blue, 1961-66; right, in ruby, 1967-81. *Collection of Glenn and Betty Close*

3.29 No. 124, green (also called empire green or emerald green) 10-in. ashtray with four raised center coins, 1963-64 (others 1960-72, but not in ruby). *Collection of Glenn and Betty Close*

3.30 Detail of green 4-coin cluster.

3.31 Detail of green coin.

3.32 Left, No. 347, green covered candy jar, H. 6 3/4 in., 1963-64 (other colors 1958-82); center, No. 680, green cream, H. 3 1/2 in., 1963-64; right, No.673, green covered sugar, H. 5 3/8 in., 1963-64. *Collection of Glenn and Betty Close*

3.33 No. 374, green cigarette box with cover, L. 5 3/4 in., W. 4 1/2 in., 1964. *Collection of Joanne Parker*

3.34 Left, No. 448, green jelly or small footed compote, H. 3 3/4 in. 1963-64; center, No. 829, tall green footed urn with cover, H. 12 3/4 in., 1963-64; right, No. 316, green 4 1/2-in. candlestick, 1963-64. *Collection of Glenn and Betty Close*

3.36 Detail of gold coins.

3.35 Gold coin on crystal, issued in 1960, was used for only four items: wedding bowl, decanter, covered candy, and cigarette box. Left, No. 347, covered candy jar, H. 6 3/4 in., 1960-70; right, No. 374, covered cigarette box, L. 5 3/4 in., W. 4 1/2 in., 1960-64; center, No. 550, crystal coin 8-in. plate, 1969-70. *Collection of Glenn and Betty Close*

3.37 Crystal coin, left, No. 400, 1-pint decanter with stopper, H. 10 3/16 in., 1960-65; center, No. 531, 7-oz. cruet with stopper, H. 6 in., 1964-70; right, No. 630, salver/cake plate, H. 6 1/2 in., D. 10 in., 1962-73. *Collection of Glenn and Betty Close*

3.38 Crystal coin, left, No. 58, 14-oz. ice tea, H. 5 5/8 in., 1969-81; top center, mystery glass (Stinson 9) H. 5 1/4 in.; bottom center, No. 73, 9-oz. water/scotch and soda, H. 4 1/4 in., 1958-70; right, No. 64, 12-oz. ice tea/high ball, H. 5 1/8 in., 1958-70. *Collection of Glenn and Betty Close*

Chapter 4

Etchings and Cuttings

Many Fostoria items are identified by a particular etching or cutting motif regardless of the design of the shape or form it is used on. In many cases, a surface decoration was used on a particular form and the two are always associated with one another. Other surface decorations can be found on a number of different forms, such as candlesticks and candelabra, which display a variety of etchings on their bases. In some instances, an intricate and very traditional motif is superimposed on an otherwise simple and modern shape. It is interesting indeed to find these unlikely combinations that did not seem to disturb either the producers or purchasers. The following is but a small sample of the amazing variety of etching and cutting decorations produced by Fostoria. An explanation of the different methods used to create these patterns can be found in the Glossary.

4.1 Cupped bowl decorated with "Spencerian O" needle etching No. 32, which was advertised in the July 8, 1891 issue of *Crockery and Glass Journal*, and with the inscription "Fostoria Glass Moundsville, W. V.;" used as a salesman sample, circa 1892, D. 4 3/4 in. *Courtesy of the Huntington Museum of Art*

4.2 No 300 blown crystal deep etched 12-in. vase, 1913-1918.
Courtesy of Kelly O'Kane

4.3 Detail of No. 300 vase.

4.4 Royal plate etching No. 273, the first dinnerware pattern to be made in color, 1925-1928; center, on No. 2329 blue 11-in. centerpiece; left and right, on No. 2324 blue 4-in. candlesticks. *Collection of Glenn and Betty Close*

4.5 Detail of No. 273 Royal plate etching.

4.6 Left, Royal on No. 869 goblet; center left, No. 5000, 9-oz. footed tumbler; center right, No. 2331/3, 7-in. round candy box with cover and three compartments; right, No. 2350, 6-in. cereal bowl, all in blue. *Collection of Glenn and Betty Close*

4.7 Center, Royal on No. 2292, 8-in. vase; left and right, No. 2324, 4-in. candlesticks, all in blue. *Collection of Glenn and Betty Close*

4.8 Top, Royal on No. 2350, 8-in. salad plate; bottom, No. 2287, 11-in. handled sandwich tray, all in amber. *Collection of Glenn and Betty Close*

4.9 Left, Royal etching on Pioneer pattern No. 2350, cup and saucer; top right, No. 2250, 1/2-lb. candy jar and cover, both in amber and produced 1926-1934; bottom, Royal on No. 2324, 4-in. candlesticks, also in amber. *Collection of Glenn and Betty Close*

4.10 Left, Royal on No. 869 goblet; center left, on No. 869 high sherbet; center, on No. 1861 1/2, 6-in. flared jelly; top right, on No. 5000, 9-oz. footed tumbler; bottom right, on No. 899 wine, all in amber. *Collection of Glenn and Betty Close*

4.11 Top, Royal on No. 2350, 7-in. plate; bottom, 2350, 10-in. baker, both in green. *Collection of Glenn and Betty Close*

4.12 Royal on No. 2287 green 11-in. handled sandwich tray. *Collection of Glenn and Betty Close*

4.13 Left, Royal on No. 869 goblet; center, No. 2250, 1/2-lb. footed candy jar with cover; right, No. 2350 cup and saucer, all in green. *Collection of Glenn and Betty Close*

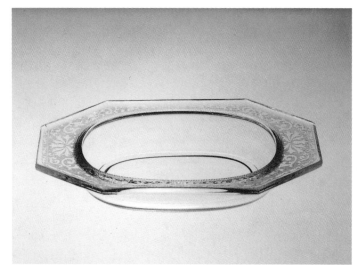

4.14 Royal on small 8-sided relish. *Collection of Grace Wilson*

4.15 Left, Royal on No. 1236-6 jug; right, on No. 2315 grapefruit, both in crystal. *Collection of Glenn and Betty Close*

4.18 Detail of Paradise etching.

4.16 Brocade plate etching No. 289 Paradise pattern, 1927-1930, on No. 4100 orchid 8-in. optic vase. *Photo courtesy of Jerry Gallagher*

4.17 Left, No. 290 Oak Leaf brocade plate etching on No. 2378 sugar pail in crystal, H. 3 5/8 in.; center, No. 289 Paradise etching on No. 4100 8-in. vase in orchid; right, No. 287 Grape etching on No. 4103 vase in rose, H. 3 1/4 in. *Courtesy of Jerry Gallagher*

4.19 Paradise pattern on No. 2362 green 11-in. compote.
Photo courtesy of Jerry Gallagher

4.20 Brocade plate etching No. 287 Grape pattern, 1927-1930,
on No. 2327 green 7-in. compote. *Photo courtesy of Jerry
Gallagher*

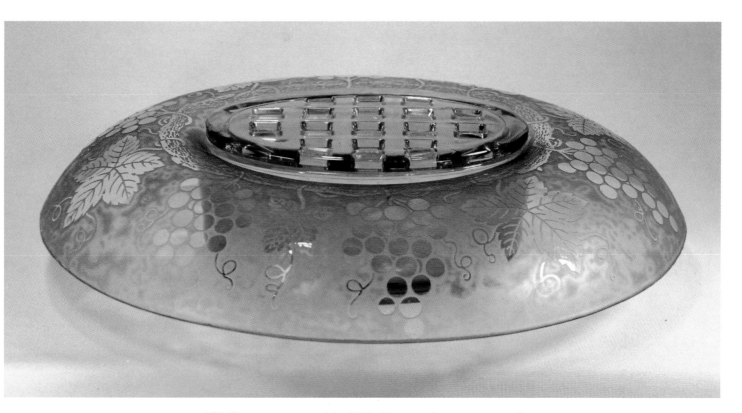

4.21 Grape pattern on No. 2371, 13-in. oval centerpiece with No. 2371 flower holder composed of crystal bowl and orchid frog, in orchid, produced 1927-1929. *Photo courtesy of Jerry Gallagher*

4.22 Grape pattern on No. 2371, 13-in. oval centerpiece with No. 2371 flower holder in green. *Photo courtesy of Jerry Gallagher*

4.23 Grape pattern on No. 4108 green 8-in. optic vase, circa 1930. *Photo courtesy of Jerry Gallagher*

4.24 Left, Oak Leaf pattern on No. 2378 whip cream pail; top center, No. 2238, 8 1/2-in. salad plate; right, No. 2394, 2-in. candleholders, all in crystal. *Photo courtesy of Jerry Gallagher*

4.25 Grape pattern on No. 2342 green 12-in. octagonal handled lunch tray. *Courtesy of Jerry Gallagher*

4.26 Brocade plate etching No. 290 Oak Leaf pattern, produced 1928-1931, on No. 2342, 12-in. octagonal handled lunch tray. *Courtesy of Jerry Gallagher*

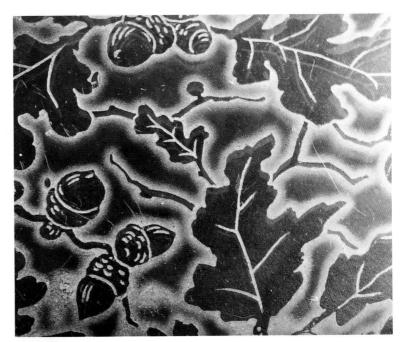

4.27 Detail of No. 290 Oak Leaf brocade plate etching.

4.28 Oak Leaf pattern on No. 2394 candleholders, 1928-1931.
Photo courtesy of Jerry Gallagher

4.29 Oak Leaf pattern on No. 2380 confection with cover in
rose. *Photo courtesy of Jerry Gallagher*

4.30 Seldom-seen plate etching No. 288 Cupid, produced
1927-1929, on No. 2297 footed bowl in green, D. 12 1/2 in.,
H. 2 1/2 in. *Courtesy of Jerry Gallagher*

4.31 Detail of Cupid.

4.32 Plate etchings designed by Edgar Bottome: Top left, Versailles No. 278 on No. 5299 high sherbet, H. 6 1/4 in.; bottom left, Versailles on 5299 cocktail, H. 5 1/8 in.; top center, June No. 279 on No. 5298, 10-oz. goblet, H. 8 1/8 in.; center, Versailles wine, H. 5 1/2 in.; top right, Versailles goblet, H. 8 1/8 in.; right, June 6-oz. high sherbet, H. 6 in., each with topaz bowl and crystal stem, circa 1931-1944. *Courtesy of Second Hand Rose Antiques*

4.33 Left, Versailles etching on No. 2375 relish, L. 8 1/2 in.; center, June etching on No. 2394 candleholder, D. 4 3/8 in.; right, Versailles on No. 2375 bonbon, L. 6 3/4 in., each in topaz, circa 1929-1938. *Courtesy of Second Hand Rose Antiques*

4.34 Detail of June plate etching No. 279.

4.35 Detail of Versailles plate etching No. 278.

4.36 Versailles on No. 5298 goblets in azure with crystal stems, 1931-1934, H. 8 1/8 in. *Collection of JoAn Jones*

4.38 Versailles on No. 2394 candle holders, H. 2 in., D. 4 3/8 in. *Collection of JoAn Jones*

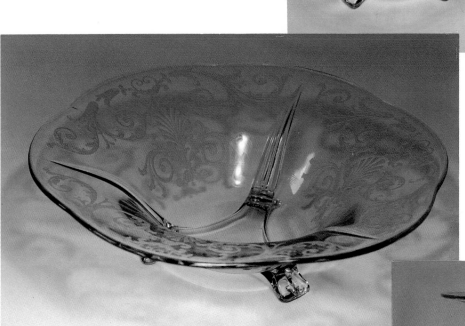

4.37 Versailles on footed center bowl in azure, 1928-1944. *Collection of JoAn Jones*

4.39 Versailles on No. 2375 azure 7-in. compote. *Collection of JoAn Jones*

Navarre Crystal
Multi-purpose Navarre Magnum.

Vichyssoise, Fresh Fruit Cup, or your favorite beverage.

Goblet · High Dessert/Champagne · Low Dessert/Champagne · Large Claret · Claret · Cordial · Brandy Inhaler

Magnum · Continental Champagne · Luncheon Goblet/Ice Tea · Footed Juice · Cocktail/Sherry · Double Old Fashioned · High Ball

4.40 Navarre plate etching No. 327, designed by Edgar Bottome and introduced in 1937, pictured in 1982 Fostoria catalog.

Navarre Giftware
Available in Crystal only.

4.41 Navarre giftware in Fostoria catalog.

4.43 Left, Navarre on No. 6016 goblet, H. 7 5/8 in.; center, 3 1/2-oz. cocktail, H. 5 1/4 in.; top right, 6-oz. saucer champagne, H. 5 5/8 in.; bottom right, 3/4-oz. cordial, H. 3 7/8 in., all in crystal.

4.42 Detail of Navarre.

4.44 Romance plate etching No. 341 in crystal, introduced in 1942 and produced into the 1980s. Left, on No. 6017, 9-oz. goblet, H. 7 3/8 in.; right, 6-oz. saucer champagne, H. 5 1/2 in. *Collection of Martha MacKenzie*

4.45 Romance on No. 2350 1/2 sugar, H. 3 1/8 in., and 7-oz. creamer, H. 3 1/4 in. *Collection of Martha MacKenzie*

4.46 No. 2594 trindle candlesticks in crystal, H. 8 in., W. 7 in., with Romance etching on base, introduced in 1942. *Collection of Martha E. MacKenzie*

4.47 Left, No. 827 cut Rose on No. 2364 shakers with metal tops; center, No. 341 Romance etching on No. 2364 shakers with glass tops; right, Seville etching on No. 5000 footed shakers in crystal with glass tops, H. 2 1/4 in. *Courtesy of Jerry Gallagher*

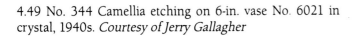

4.48 Left, No. 2375 shakers in green with Versailles etching; center, in crystal with Meadow Rose etching; right, in azure, H. 3 1/4 in. *Courtesy of Jerry Gallagher*

4.49 No. 344 Camellia etching on 6-in. vase No. 6021 in crystal, 1940s. *Courtesy of Jerry Gallagher*

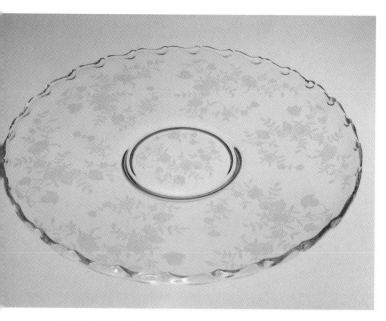

4.50 No. 2630 Century 10 1/2-in. snack tray with No. 342 Bouquet etching. *Collection of Grace Wilson*

4.52 Holly cutting No. 815, combination of grey and polished cutting on No. 2364 handled lunch tray, produced 1941-1980s, D. 11 1/4 in. *Courtesy of Rae Hamilton*

4.51 Century handled lunch tray with No. 833 Bridal Wreath cutting, D. 11 1/4 in. *Collection of Grace Wilson*

4.53 Holly cutting on No. 2364 centerpiece bowl or lily pond, D. 12 in. *Courtesy of Rae Hamilton*

4.54 Left, Holly on No. 2364, 2-part relish, L. 6 1/2 in., W. 5 in.; right, Holly on No. 2364, 3-part relish, L. 10 in., W. 7 1/4 in. *Courtesy of Rae Hamilton*

4.55 Left, Holly on No. 2350 1/2, 7-oz. footed creamer, H. 3 1/4 in.; top right, Holly on No. 2350 1/2 footed sugar, H. 3 1/8 in.; bottom, No. 2350 oval pickle dish, L. 8 in. *Courtesy of Rae Hamilton*

4.56 Holly on No. 6030 stemware; left, 10-oz. goblet, H. 7 7/8 in.; center, 5-oz. footed tumbler, H. 4 5/8 in.; right, 6-oz. saucer champagne, H. 5 5/8 in., produced from the 1940s through the 1970s. *Courtesy of Rae Hamilton*

Chapter 5

Variety and Color

One of the most impressive features of the Fostoria Glass Company was its versatility. From Victorian pattern glass to delicately colored and etched stemware, from traditional forms and decorations to the simplicity of Art Deco, Fostoria delivered variety. It is no wonder that a company that catered to and directed consumer tastes for nearly a century was able to take advantage of numerous forming methods, decorating techniques and styles. A look at some examples from this repertoire is like seeing a short history of American production glass of this century.

Categorizing Fostoria can be done in several ways. Chronological order can be confusing, because some patterns were taken out of production much sooner than others. If a design was popular, it remained in production long after it was introduced; the American pattern is an extreme example of this. Certain classifications seem to be more natural than others: Victorian pattern glass made primarily in Fostoria, Ohio; a later version of pattern glass, Coin; etchings; and the overwhelmingly popular pattern, American. These have each been considered in other chapters. Another, perhaps unlikely, category for Fostoria is "modern," and that has been moved to a separate chapter as well. What remains can, of course, be further divided but instead has been ordered somewhat chronologically into this chapter. What follows is a sample of some of the delightful variety produced over the years.

5.1 Partial display of Fostoria glass at the Huntington Museum of Art, Huntington, West Virginia.

5.2 Fostoria glass at the Huntington Museum of Art.

5.3 Pressed 8-inch berry bowl, No. 794, pictured in 1901 catalog, also available in 7-inch and 4 1/2-inch sizes, produced pre-1900 to about 1904. *Courtesy of the Huntington Museum of Art*

794 8 inch Berry. Packed 3 doz. in bbl.
Made also in 7 inch

5.4 Illustration of No. 794 in 1901 catalog.

5.5 Round covered butter dish, No. 440, St. Bernard pattern circa 1893, D. 8 in. The dog motif is found on the lid of sugar bowl, butter dish, and high compotes (or comports) as well as at the base of the berry bowl and flat pickle dish. (Kamm 507) Fostoria's first mold maker Charles E. Beam was known for his novelties, such as covered animal dishes, so it is likely that he was responsible for this design. *Courtesy of the Huntington Museum of Art*

5.6 Butter dish with lid removed to show the dog in the center of the dish as well as the finial on the cover.

5.7 Relish or pickle dish in St. Bernard pattern, No. 450. *Courtesy of the Huntington Museum of Art*

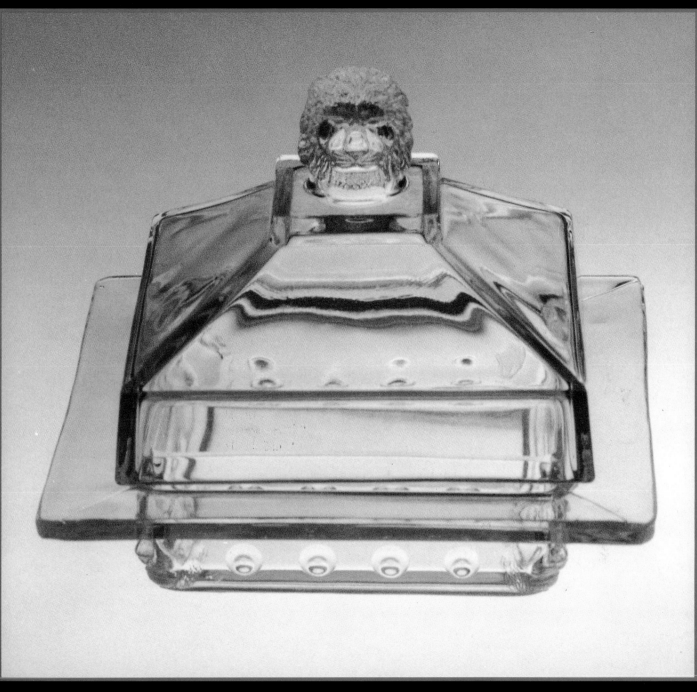

5.8 Square covered dish in Atlanta pattern, No. 500, circa 1895, discontinued for the most part by 1897. The double-faced lion head, variously called Atlanta Lion, Lion Head, and Lion Mask, is used as a finial and knob on covered pieces; a single lion face is on the corners at the base of square pieces; all were made clear, frosted, or a combination of both. *Courtesy of the Huntington Museum of Art*

5.9 Robin Hood pattern, No. 603, produced from about 1898 to 1903 of pressed soda-lime glass. Left, crystal salver, D. 10 1/2 in.; right, green creamer, H. 4 3/8 in., probably made at a later date when colors were popular. *Courtesy of the Huntington Museum of Art*

603   9-inch Salver.   Packed 1¼ doz. in bbl.
603 10-inch Salver.   Packed 1   doz. in bbl.

Cream. Packed 8 doz. in bbl.

5.10 Illustrations of Robin Hood creamer and salver in 1901 catalog.

5.11 Robin Hood, No. 603, mug of pressed soda lime glass, H. 3 1/8 in.

5.13 Front view of No. 618 jug.

5.12 No. 618, 3-pint jug, pre-1898 to 1910, advertised as extra fire polished and pictured in the 1901 catalog, H. 10 in. This has probably been reproduced recently since it is often found with sloppy seams at bargain prices. *Courtesy of Verna Polley*

618 3-pint Jug. Packed 2½ doz. in bbl.

5.14 Illustration of No. 618 jug in 1901 catalog.

5.15 Left, cruet No. 1660, of pressed colorless soda lime glass, circa 1909-1922; right, 1/2-gal. jug also pattern No, 1660, H. 8 1/2 in.; center, finger bowl in No. 501 Hartford pattern, circa 1898-1901, though in green may be of a later date, D. 5 in. *Courtesy of the Huntington Museum of Art*

5.16 Left, Louise, No. 1121, tumbler circa 1902-1907; center left, vase No. 504, designed by Phillip Ebeling with pattern faux cut, or pressed to appear cut (also described as etched and intaglio cut) with panels cut flat, 1900-1910, H. 4 3/4 in.; center right, shaker also in No. 504, H. 3 1/2 in.; right, candlestick No. 1964, plate etched decoration, 1920-1925, H. 9 1/4 in. *Courtesy of the Huntington Museum of Art*

5.17 Tumbler in Flemish pattern No. 1913, designed by Phillip Ebeling in 1913 and produced until 1928, and similer to another of his designs, the No. 2222 Colonial. which, in turn, is similar to Heisey's Colonial pattern of 1897. *Courtesy of the Huntington Musuem of Art*

5.18 Spooner in Lucere pattern No. 1515, found in the Fostoria morgue and probably an experimental color or made at a late date than the 1907-1915 of Lucere production, H. 4 in. *Courtesy of the Huntington Museum of Art*

5.19 Compotes in Lucere pattern No. 1515, also found in Fostoria morgue and probably from a later date using the old molds, left D. 6 1/2 in. *Courtesy of the Huntington Musuem of Art*

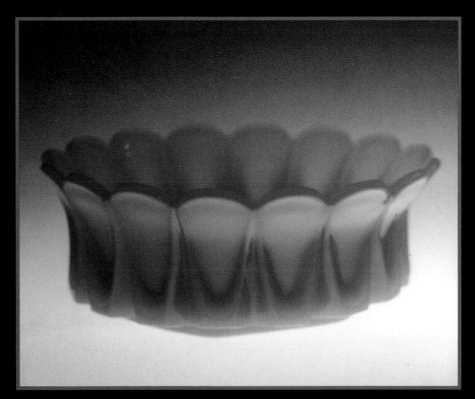

5.20 Compote in Long Buttress pattern No. 1299, produced 1904-1913, this example in an experimental color or made at a later date, made in 4, 5, 7, 8, and 9-in. sizes, this one measuring 9 3/8 in. *Courtesy of the Huntington Museum of Art.*

5.21 Humidor in Long Buttress No. 1299, with silver-plated cover, H. 6 1/2 in. *Courtesy of the Huntington Museum of Art*

5.22 "Art Decorated" vase with American Indian portrait, H. 7 1/2 in. A series of mold blown vases and mugs were contracted and distributed by Butler Bros. from about 1900 to 1910. They were made of milk glass and sprayed with shaded brown, terra cotta, or green backgrounds and decorated with transfer prints of native American Indians and other subjects, such as monks or Arabs. (Warner 18) Liebmann illustrates ten different Indian portraits that were used on nine different vase shapes. (Liebman 22-23) *Courtesy of the Huntington Musuem of Art*

5.23 Art Decorated vase in green with brown transfer print of American Indian, 1900-1910, H. 7 1/4 in. *Collection of Joanne Parker*

5.24 Detail of Indian on green vase.

5.25 Milk glass vase with hand-painted floral decoration, mounted as a ewer with metal base, handle, and spout, H. 18 in. *Collection of Joanne Parker*

5.26 Smaller ewer, also of hand decorated milk glass with metal mounts, H. 12 in. *Collection of Joanne Parker*

5.27 Similar floral ewer, probably by Fostoria. *Collection of Vicki Christensen*

5.28 Toothpick in No. 1630 Alexis pattern originally produced 1909-1925. Founding members of the Fostoria Glass Society of America each received one of these new issues with a molded inscription at the base, FGSA 1980. *Collection of Joanne Parker*

5.29 No. 1630 Alexis commercial line tumbler made for Dripping Springs Whiskey, H. 3 7/8 in. *Courtesy of Jerry Gallagher*

5.30 Left, Alexis flat table salt, D. 2 7/8 in.; center, high foot bowl, H. 5 1/2 in.; right, footed individual salt, H. 2 3/8 in. *Salts courtesy of Jerry Gallagher*

5.31 No. 2321 Mah Jongg Set produced 1925-1928 consisting of 5 1/2-oz. sherbet in amber with blue enamel decoration on foot, H. 3 1/2 in., on amber plate with blue enamel rim and molded ring to hold sherbet, D. 8 1/2 in. *Courtesy of Jerry Gallagher*

5.32 Mah Jongg Set, green plate with orange enamel rim and green sherbet with orange enamel foot; sets also came in crystal, canary, and ebony. *Courtesy of Jerry Gallagher*

5.33 No. 2440 Lafayette in Wisteria (light lavender color produced 1931-1938). Left, 5 1/2-oz. sherbet/saucer champagne with crystal stem and Wisteria bowl, produced 1933-1935, on 8-in salad plate; center, No. 6004, 9-oz. goblet with Wisteria bowl; right, cup and saucer. *Photo courtesy of Jerry Gallagher*

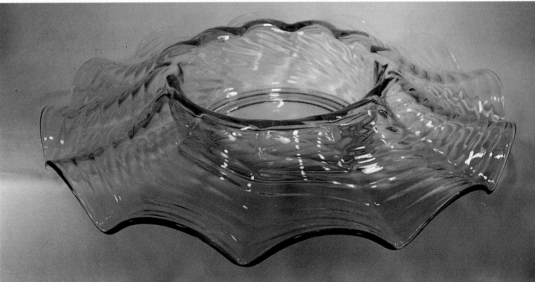

5.34 No. 2393 azure 12-in. centerpiece, 1928-1931. *Collection of Bunny Benedict, photo Jerry Gallagher*

5.35 Left, No. 870 cocktail; right, No. 5084 oyster cocktail, late 1920s in blue. *Collection of Mary Frances Pausch, photo Jerry Gallagher*

5.36 No. 5298 goblets with green bowl and crystal base, early 1930s.

5.37 Left, No. 6007 footed tumbler in topaz, H. 5 1/4 in., 1931-44; top center, No. 6005, 9-oz. goblet with amber stem, 1931-44; bottom center, No. 4095 blue-footed almond with crystal bowl, H. 1 5/8 in.; right, No. 6007 cocktail in wisteria, H. 4 5/8 in., 1931-44. *Courtesy of Jerry Gallagher*

5.38 Left, No. 2375 Fairfax bon bon in azure, produced 1928-1941, L. 6 3/4 in.; right, No. 5299 low sherbet in azure, H. 4 1/8 in. *Courtesy of Second Hand Rose Antiques*

5.39 Sun Ray No. 2510 five-piece condiment set consisting of 3-oz. oil and vinegar, two covered mustard jars with spoons, on four-lobed tray, L. 8 1/2 in., produced 1935-1944. *Courtesy of the Huntington Museum of Art*

5.40 Left, Sun Ray 3-part relish; right, handled nappy. *Collection of Grace Wilson*

5.41 Sun Ray handled bowl, L. 14 in.

5.42 Left, No. 2470 footed vase in lavender optic with crystal base, circa 1930s, H. 10 in.; right, gourd-shaped optic vase; center, late cigarette box purchased at the factory just before closing in 1986. *Courtesy of the Huntington Museum of Art*

5.43 No. 2276 Vanity Set combination perfume and powder jar with encrusted gold decoration, produced 1924-1930; left, copper blue with plain gold bands and crystal stopper, H. 7 3/4 in.; right, pink with encrusted gold. Patent was filed on Jan. 10, 1923 by its creator, Harry G. Dalzell. *Collection of Vicki Christensen*

5.44 No. 2351 cigarette holder in crystal with azure stem and cupped base, produced about 1925-1930. *Courtesy of the Huntington Museum of Art*

5.45 No. 5092 cigarette holder in crystal with azure stem and cupped base, about 1925-1930, also made in rose, green, and amber. *Photo courtesy of Jerry Gallagher*

5.46 Left No. 2449 Hermitage goblet, H. 5 1/4 in., right, No. 2449 1/2 shot glass, H. 2 1/2 in., both in crystal, 1932-45. *Courtesy of Jerry Gallagher*

5.47 No. 2449 1/2 Hermitage 6-oz. old fashioned/cocktails in wisteria, topaz, green and azure, H. 3 1/4 in., 1932-42. *Courtesy of Jerry Gallagher*

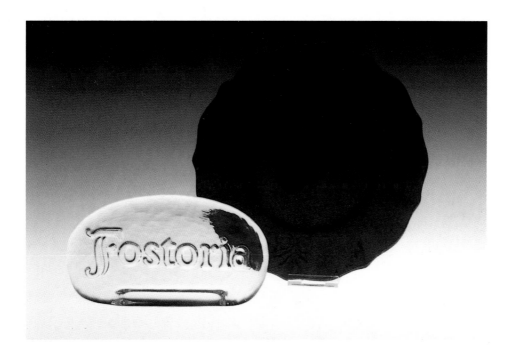

5.48 Fostoria logo and Baroque plate with label on back written "batch 458 royal blue color – experimental," D. 7 3/8 in. *Courtesy of the Huntington Museum of Art*

5.49 No. 2496 Baroque 12-in. flared bowl in topaz, 1936-38. *Collection of Grace Wilson*

5.50 Topaz Baroque, 1936-38: left, handled flared nappy, D. 5 in., center, 5 1/2 in. compote, H. 4 3/4 in.; right, No. 2496 1/2 mayonnaise (comes with plate), H. 3 1/2 in. *Collection of Grace Wilson*

5.51 Topaz Baroque: top, dinner plate; center, footed cup and saucer; bottom, salad plate. *Collection of Grace Wilson*

5.52 Baroque: top, crystal 3-toed tid bit, D. 8 1/4 in., 1936-66; bottom left, azure footed cream, 1936-44; bottom center, topaz covered mustard; right, crystal mustard. *Collection of Grace Wilson*

5.53 Left, Baroque ice bucket with metal handles; right, footed sugar. *Collection of Grace Wilson*

5.54 left, Baroque footed dish; right, 6 1/2-in. compote in crystal with No. 329 Lido plate etching, 1937-55. *Collection of Grace Wilson*

5.55 Baroque shakers with glass tops: left, azure; right, individual in amber. *Photo courtesy of Jerry Gallagher*

5.56 Left, Baroque trindle candlestick with silver deposit, 8 1/4-in. spread; right, duo candlestick with 8-in. spread. *Collection of Grace Wilson*

5.57 Baroque 4-in. single candlesticks. *Collection of Grace Wilson*

5.58 No. 2545 Flame lustres in crystal, 1936-1944. *Collection of Grace Wilson*

5.59 Century No. 2630 (produced 1949-1985) stemware and giftware from 1982 Fostoria catalog.

Top: No. 2, 10 1/2-oz. goblet, H. 5 3/4 in; No. 7, 5 1/2-oz. sherbet, H. 4 1/4 in.; No. 26, 3 1/2-oz. wine, H. 4 1/2 in.; No. 63, 12-oz. ice tea, H. 5 7/8 in.; No. 550, 8-in. plate; No. 549, 7-in. plate; No. 350, candy jar and cover, H. 7 in.; No. 836, oval vegetable dish, L. 9 1/2 in.; No. 540, 8 3/4-in. pickle dish; No. 211, large 10-in. bowl on No. 567, 14-in. torte plate; No. 707, 3-toed tid bit, D. 8 1/8 in.; No. 300, oblong butter and cover.

Bottom: No. 316, 4 1/2-in. candlestick; No. 204, oval utility bowl, L. 10 in.; No. 650, individual shaker with chrome top C, H. 2 3/8 in.; No. 649, shaker with chrome top B, H. 3 1/4 in.; No. 512, 6-in. small bowl; No. 396-397, footed cup and saucer; No. 499, 4 1/2-in. handled nappy; No. 622, 3-part relish, L. 11 1/8 in.; No. 620, 2-part relish, L. 7 3/8 in.; No. 306, handled cake plate, D. 9 1/2 in.

5.60 Century 3-part relish with SAMPLE etched so it would not be sold; if the sample item was well received, production could begin. L. 11 1/8 in., W. 8 1/2 in.

5.61 Left, Century 10 1/2-oz. goblets, H. 5 3/4 in.; right, 3-pint ice jug, H. 7 1/8 in. *Collection of Robert McKeand*

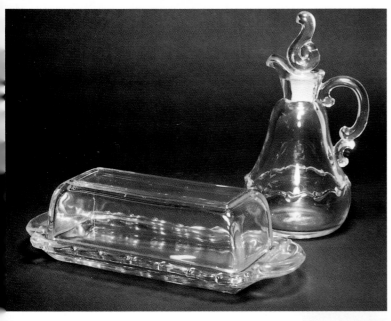

5.62 Left, oblong butter and cover, L. 7 1/2 in.; right, 5-oz oil with stopper, H. 6 in. *Collection of Robert McKeand*

5.63 Century No. 648 handled serving dish, H. 3 1/4 in. and shakers with chrome lids, H. 3 1/3 in. *Collection of Robert McKeand*

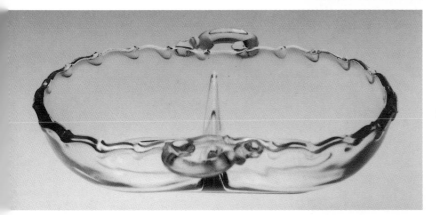

5.64 Century 2-part relish with handles, L. 7 3/8 in.

5.65 Unusual 2-part relish with pressed design on bottom, L. 9 3/8 in.

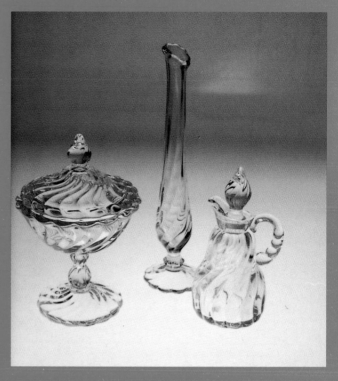

5.66 No. 2412 Colony introduced in 1938 as a later issue of Cascade and Queen Anne, 2-qt. ice jug, H. 7 3/4 in. *Collection of Grace Wilson*

5.67 Left, Colony jelly and cover, 1949-60; center, bud vase; right, 4-oz. oil with stopper, H. 5 7/8 in., 1940-59. *Collection of Grace Wilson*

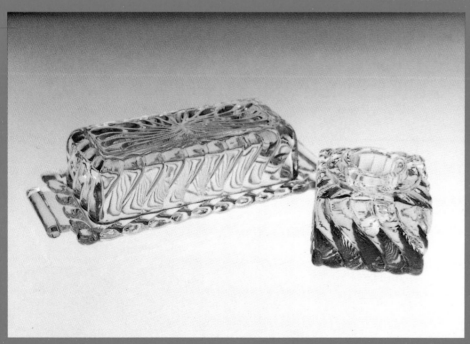

5.68 Left, Colony oblong butter and cover, L. 7 1/2 in., 1949-72; right, probably an early Cascade inkwell without lid. *Collection of Grace Wilson*

5.69 Left, Colony 4-oz. oyster coctail, H. 3 3/8 in., 1940-72; center, 5-oz. sherbet, H. 3 5/8 in., 1940-79; right, 3 1/2-oz. cocktail, H. 4 in., 1940-72. *Collection of Grace Wilson*

5.70 Left, Colony 5-oz. footed juice, H. 4 1/2 in.; right, 9-oz. goblet, H. 5 1/8 in., both 1940-79. *Collection of Grace Wilson*

5.71 Left, Colony 2412 1/2, 9-oz. tumbler, H. 4 7/8 in., 1940-76; right, 9-oz. tumbler, H. 3 7/8 in., 1940-72. *Collection of Grace Wilson*

5.72 Colony 6-in. rose bowl, 1949-60. *Collection of Grace Wilson*

5.74 Colony 13-in. torte plate, 1941-1973. *Collection of Grace Wilson*

5.73 Colony 7 1/2-in. flared vase, 1940-60. *Collection of Grace Wilson*

5.75 Colony individual sugar and cream, H. 3 1/2 in., on tray, L. 6 3/4 in., 1940-1971. *Collection of Grace Wilson*

5.76 Left, Colony 7 1/2-in. lustre, 1938-60; right, 7-in. candlestick, 1939-73. *Collection of Grace Wilson*

5.78 Left, No. 5412 Colonial Dame 12-oz. luncheon goblet, H. 6 in.; right, 3 1/2-oz. cocktail, H. 4 in., both with empire green bowl and crystal base, introduced 1948. *Photo courtesy of Jerry Gallagher*

5.77 Colony 3-in. candlesticks, 1940-60. *Collection of Grace Wilson*

5.79 Colonial Dame 6 1/2-oz. sherbet, H. 4 5/8 in. *Collection of Grace Wilson*

5.80 No. 6149 Maypole, a colored reissue of Colony in 1982, bud vases in light blue, ruby, crystal, and peach, H. 6 3/4 in. *Collection of Grace Wilson*

5.82 Small bowl in light turquoise milk glass with FOSTORIA paper label. *Collection of Grace Wilson*

5.81 No. 2412 candy box with cover in milk glass, D. 6 1/2 in., 1954-65. *Collection of Grace Wilson*

5.83 No. 2678 Monroe pattern 10 1/2-in. shallow bowl in white milk glass (identical to banana bowl but without the foot) 1950s-1965. *Collection of Grace Wilson*

5.84 No. 2678 Monroe footed fruit bowl in white milk glass. *Collection of Grace Wilson*

5.85 Ebony 4-in. candlesticks. *Collection of Joanne Parker*

5.86 Left, milk glass tumbler; right, No. 827/842 Jenny Lind cologne flask with stopper, 1961-1965, H. 10 3/4 in. *Courtesy of the Huntington Musuem of Art*

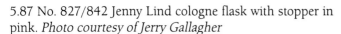

5.87 No. 827/842 Jenny Lind cologne flask with stopper in pink. *Photo courtesy of Jerry Gallagher*

5.88 Detail of Jenny Lind box top.

5.89 No. 833/293 Jenny Lind jewel box and cover in blue, 1961-1965, L. 6 in. *Collection of Vicki Christensen*

5.90 Blue Jenny Lind, 1961-1965: top, No. 832/287 glove box and cover, L. 10 3/8 in.; bottom left, No. 831/276 handkerchief box and cover, W. 5 1/4 in.; bottom right, No. 828/281 pin box and cover, L. 5 in. *Collection of Joanne Parker*

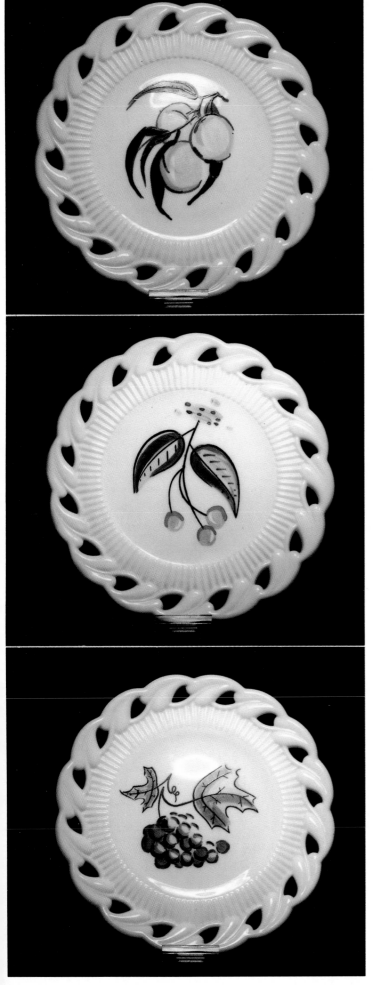

Top left: 5.91 No. 2620 Betsy Ross 8-in. plate in milk glass with enamel decoration No. 523, hand painted peaches, early 1960s. *Collection of Glenn and Betty Close*

Center Left: 5.92 No. 2620 with enamel decoration No. 523, cherries. *Collection of Glenn and Betty Close*

Bottom Left: 5.93 No. 2620 with enamel decoration No. 523, grapes. *Collection of Glenn and Betty Close*

Top Right: 5.94 No. 2620 with enamel decoration No. 523, pears. *Collection of Glenn and Betty Close*

Center Right: 5.95 No. 2620 with enamel decoration No. 523, apples. *Collection of Glenn and Betty Close*

5.96 Argus, Jamestown, Moonstone, and Virginia casual stemware in Fostoria catalog.

Argus Ruby

By special arrangement with the Henry Ford Museum

Tumbler High Ball

Casual Stemware

Goblet

Sherbet

Wine

Luncheon Goblet/Ice Tea

Tumbler Old Fashioned

Dessert

Juice/ Cocktail

Crystal Goblet

Olive Green Goblet

Jamestown Pink

Goblet

Sherbet

Footed Juice

Wine

Luncheon Goblet/ Ice Tea

Ruby Goblet

Amber Goblet

Blue Goblet

Brown Goblet

Moonstone Dark Blue

Goblet

Sherbet

Wine

Luncheon Goblet/ Ice Tea

Light Blue Goblet

Taupe Goblet

Yellow Goblet

Green Goblet

Pink Goblet

Virginia Light Blue

Goblet

Sherbet

Wine

Luncheon Goblet Ice Tea

Brown Goblet

Dark Blue Goblet

Green Goblet

11

5.97 Jamestown No. 2719, designed by George Sakier,
produced 1958-1985, and pictured in 1979 brochure.

Jamestown
Made in
Green
Blue
Brown
Ruby
Amber
Pink

5.98 Left, Jamestown footed juice in smoke, H. 4 3/4 in.; right,
amber goblet, H. 5 3/4 in. *Collection of Grace Wilson*

5.99 Left rear, 11-oz. ice tea in amber; H. 6 in.; front center, 5-oz. footed juice in amethyst, H. 4 3/8 in.; assortment of 9 1/2 oz. goblets in blue, green crystal, brown, and pink. *Collection of Joanne Parker*

5.100 Jamestown No. 2719/653 shakers with chrome top A, H. 3 1/2 in., with 4-oz. ruby wine. *Collection of Joanne Parker*

5.101 Left, Jamestown No. 2719/447 jelly and cover in amber, produced 1958-1965, H. 6 1/8 in.; right, No. 2719/456, 3-pint ice jug in brown, produced 1961-1970, H. 7 5/16 in. *Collection of Joanne Parker*

5.102 Argus No. 2770 of the Henry Ford Museum collection,
produced from the 1960s to 1985 (and being produced again
today), pictured in a 1979 brochure.

5.103 Argus 12-oz. tumbler/highballs in olive green, H. 5 1/4
in. *Collection of Grace Wilson*

5.104 Argus 10 1/2-oz. goblets in ruby, H. 6 1/2 in. *Collection of Joanne Parker*

5.105 Argus 10 1/2-oz. goblet in olive green, H. 6 1/2 in. *Collection of Jerry Gallagher*

5.106 Regal decoration No. 693, a stainless steel overlay on No. 6092 Priscilla stem shapes, circa 1970s. Left, No. 27, 4-oz wine/cocktail; center left, No. 2, 10 1/2-oz. goblet; center right, No. 11, 7-oz. sherbet; right, No. 63, 14-oz. footed ice tea; top center, cocktail mixer probably from another company. *Photo courtesy of Jerry Gallagher*

5.107 Regal stems. *Courtesy of Jerry Gallagher*

5.108 Little pitcher made for Avon in 1976 with Mt. Vernon on oval emblem to commemorate the Bicentennial. Avon pieces were produced in cobalt; this rare crystal example was a first run proof, not sold commercially, H. 5 1/2 in. *Collection of Joanne Parker*

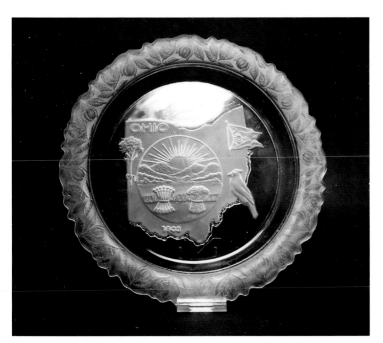

5.109 Avon goblet in cobalt blue with George Washington medallion, H. 8 in.

5.110 Our American States plate No. 2838/552, Ohio in a limited edition of 3,000, D. 10 1/2 in. *Collection of Glenn and Betty Close*

5.113 Left, No. 2632 frosted amber duck, H. 4 in.; center, No. 2531 ebony pelican made in 1993 for the Fostoria Glass Society of America, H. 4 1/2 in.; right, No. 2632 green duck. *Collection of Joanne Parker*

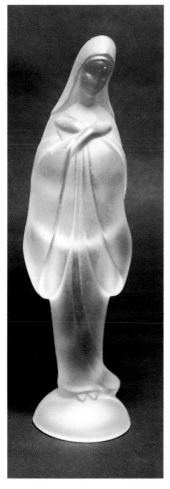

5.114 Top left and right, No. 2631/702 and 703 amber squirrels, H. 3 1/8 and 2 5/8; top center, 2632/406 walking duck, H. 2 3/8 in.; bottom, No. 452 frosted and regular blue ladybugs designed by Jon Saffell in 1970. *Collection of Joanne Parker*

5.111 No. 2715/469 Saint Francis figure with No. 525 silver mist finish, circa 1960s, H. 13 1/2 in. *Collection of Joanne Parker*

5.112 No. 2635 Madonna figure with silver mist finish, H. 10 in. *Courtesy of Jerry Gallagher*

5.115 No. 6125 Distinction blown lead glass stemware with blue bowl and crystal base, 1972-1985. Left, No. 2, 11-oz. goblet, H. 7 1/8 in.; right, No. 26, 6 1/2 oz. wine, H. 6 1/4 in. *Courtesy of Sharon Ferchill*

5.116 Hurricanes with candle well visible below the globe, with original shipping box labeled 2796 vase, in Morgantown colors Peacock Blue and Gypsy Fire, H. 16 1/2 in. *Photo courtesy of Jerry Gallagher*

5.117 No. 2887 Heritage highball in lead crystal, 1970s-85, H. 5 1/2 in.

Chapter 6

Mostly Modern

When one thinks of Fostoria, images of delicately etched-flowers on softly-colored or crystal stemware and other tableware usually come to mind. Perhaps the icecube motif of the American line, or the deeply pressed patterns of the Victorian era come to mind as well. One term that is probably not associated with Fostoria glass is "modern," because the majority of the glass was intentionally and consistently traditional in style. Yet from the 1920s and 1930s came several distinctly Art Deco designs, some with a modernized classicism. Later, the freeform shapes of the 1950s and 1960s were apparent in items of the Heirloom pattern, even though other items have a much earlier influence.

The title of this chapter, Mostly Modern, does concede that Fostoria's venture into modernism was still a bit tentative and sometimes oddly eclectic. The bases of some of the candlesticks and candelabra are often found with some of the most traditional etchings superimposed onto otherwise bold sculptural forms. Items in the opalescent Homespun and Needlepoint lines of the 1950s seem modern in the respect that they are new and different, but some might argue, not quite new and different enough. Nevertheless, the range of designs in this mostly modern category would indicate that Fostoria did more than dabble. Some rather innovative, if not radical, designs were produced concurrently with their mainstay of traditional patterns. Some of these atypical items may come as a surprise even to those familiar with Fostoria.

6.1 No. 2297 green 7-in. candlesticks, 1924-28., H. 7 1/4 in.

6.2a No. 2288 Tut vase in green, 1924-28, H. 8 3/8 in.

6.2b Green Tut vase with cut decoration that seems to have no relation to the style of the vase. *Collection of Grace Wilson*

6.3 Left, ice bucket, D. 5 3/4 in.; center, No. 2321 Pricilla jug in blue, 1925-1930, H. 9 3/4 in.; right, Pricilla footed tumbler with handle (also made without handle), H. 6 1/8 in. *Courtesy of the Huntington Museum of Art*

6.4 Left, No. 2297 covered jar with three feet, in green, 1924-1928; center, No. 2327 amber 7-in. compote, 1924-28, also made in crystal, blue, canary, and green; right, No. 2378 amber sugar pail, 1928-1933. *Courtesy of the Huntington Museum of Art*

6.5 No. 2419 Mayfair compote in green with Art Deco flavor, 1930-31. *Photo courtesy of Jerry Gallagher*

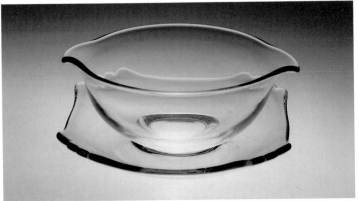

6.6 Mayfair sauce bowl with attached stand in topaz, bowl D. 5 1/2 in., 1930-38. *Courtesy of Jerry Gallagher*

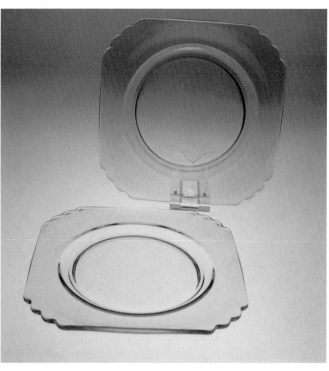

6.7 Mayfair wisteria, 1930-42: top, bonbon, D. 6 1/4 in.; bottom, sugar, H. 2 5/8 in., and cream, H. 3 1/4 in. *Courtesy of Jerry Gallagher*

6.8 Mayfair 7-in. plates in green and amber.

6.9 Collection of Art Deco vases designed by George Sakier, circa 1930, in azure, green, dawn, topaz, orchid, amber, ebony, crystal, and silver mist, ranging in height from 6 to 13 inches. *Photo courtesy of Christie's New York*

6.10 Covered bowl in modern classical form in green, possibly No. 2395, circa 1930. *Photo courtesy of Jerry Gallagher*

6.11 Left, 9-in. lustre with ebony base and crystal top and prisms, H. 8 3/4 in.; right, No. 2299 ebony clock case, H. 5 3/4 in., both circa late 1920s to early 1930s. *Courtesy of the Huntington Museum of Art*

6.12 Whirlpool cutting No. 730, (1934-1940) on No. 6011 saucer champagne with reeded stem.

6.13 Spinet cutting No. 821 on No. 6033 low sherbet, H. 4 in.

6.14 No. 2518 decanter and whiskeys in cobalt or regal blue, 1934-38. *Photo courtesy of Jerry Gallagher*

6.15 No. 4113 candlestick in regal blue, H. 6 in., 1936-44. *Courtesy of Jerry Gallagher*

6.16 Needlepoint No. 4184/84 mold-blown opalescent 8-oz. juice/old fashioned in gold (also made in moss-green and teal-blue), circa 1955, H. 3 1/16 in. with etched mark on base FOSTORIA.

6.17 Needlepoint No. 4184/58 opalescent 16 1/2-oz. ice tea in amber, H. 5 1/2 in. with 8-oz. juice, both circa 1950s with etched mark, FOSTORIA on base.

6.18 Homespun No. 4183/58 mold blown opalescent 15-oz. ice tea/highball in moss green, circa 1954, H. 5 11/16 in. with etched mark FOSTORIA. *Courtesy of the Huntington Musuem of Art*

6.19 Homespun opalescent 11 1/2-oz. water/scotch & soda in teal blue, H. 4 11/16, with etched mark, FOSTORIA.

6.20 Left, Homespun juice/old fashioned in moss green, H. 3 1/16 in.; right, Heirloom No. 2728/751 opalescent 4 1/2-in. handled vase, produced 1959-1970. *Courtesy of the Huntington Museum of Art*

6.21 No. 2727/239 Heirloom crimped bowl in opalescent
pink, D. 11 in. *Courtesy of American Antiques*

6.22 View of Heirloom crimped bowl.

6.23 No. 1515 Heirloom bowl in pink opalescent, 1960s. *Collection of Grace Wilson*

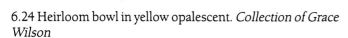
6.24 Heirloom bowl in yellow opalescent. *Collection of Grace Wilson*

6.25 Heirloom bowl in blue opalescent. *Collection of Grace Wilson*

6.26 Heirloom 2720 Florette square in blue opalescent, 5 3/8 in.

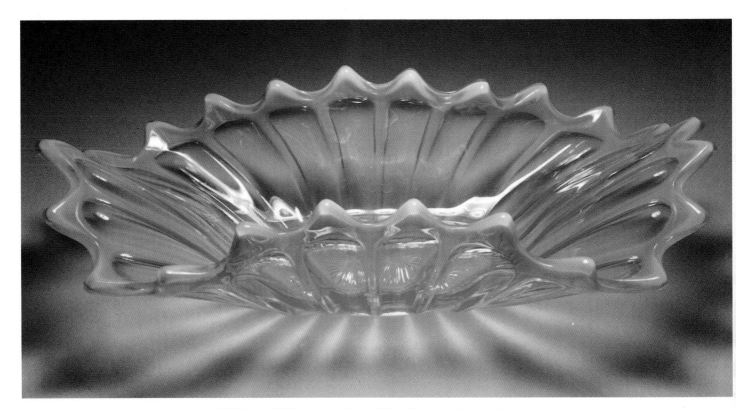

6.27 No. 1515 Heirloom 15-in. oblong bowl in blue opalescent.
Collection of Grace Wilson

6.28 No. 1515 Heirloom 15-in. oblong bowl in orange.
Collection of Joanne Parker

6.29 No. 2729 Heirloom white opalescent bonbon, circa
1960s, L. 7 in., W. 5 1/2 in. *Collection of Joanne Parker*

6.30 No. 2729 Heirloom bonbon in blue, L. 7 in. *Collection
of Grace Wilson*

6.31 Roulette No. 2739 trident vase in ruby and crystal, (also made in ebony and crystal), H. 5 1/2 in., ave. L. 8 1/2 in.

6.32 Left, Seascape No. 2685, blue opalescent candleholder, 1954-58, H. 2 in., D. 4 1/2 in.; center, No. 2660 flip vase, H. 9 in.; right, No. 684 Moonmist, silver mist decorated stem, 1969- 1972, on 10-oz. sherbet (in same shape used for No. 683 Versailles etching), H. 5 1/2 in. with paper label FOSTORIA MOONMIST. *Courtesy of the Huntington Museum of Art*

6.33 Seascape cream and sugar in blue opalescent.

6.34 Top, Seascape 8-in. shallow bowl; bottom 10-in. salad bowl in blue opalescent.

6.35 No. 6144 Lotus stemware in crystal with ebony base, 1980-1985, pictured on 1979 Brochure.

6.37 Lotus Ebony 10-oz. clarets, H. 7 1/4 in. with Fostoria logo. *Collection of Joanne Parker*

New Classics
Lotus Crystal Mist

*Luncheon Goblet/Ice Tea,
Large Claret, Goblet,
Dessert/Champagne*

Lotus Ebony

Goblet   *Dessert/
Champagne*   *Large Claret*   *Luncheon
Goblet/
Ice Tea*

6.36 Lotus Crystal Mint and Lotus Ebony stemware.

6.38 Left, Lotus Ebony 8-oz. champagne, H. 6 1/2 in.; right, 11-oz. goblet, H. 8 1/4 in. *Collection of Joanne Parker*

6.39 Left, No. 6030 Contrast cordial (called Eloquence if not black and white), 1970s, H. 3 1/2 in.; center, Contrast goblet also with black base and white bowl, H. 7 in.; right, No. 6011 Neo Classic cordial in ruby, H. 3 1/4 in. *Courtesy of Jerry Gallagher*

6.40 No. 2825 Seashells in copper blue, designed by Helena Tynell, 1971-1973.

6.41 Russel Wright designs for Fostoria, 1946-1948, but not commercially produced. *Courtesy of the Huntington Museum of Art*

6.42 Bowls, possibly designed by Russel Wright for Fostoria, found in the "morgue," the catch-all storage place for miscellaneous pieces of glass from other companies as well as Fostoria experiments. *Courtesy of the Huntington Museum of Art*

6.43 Bowl and tumbler from the Fostoria morgue, possibly designed by Russel Wright. *Courtesy of the Huntington Museum of Art*

6.44 Short brown and tall white candleholders with textured and frosted finish, probably Fostoria. *Courtesy of the Huntington Museum of Art*

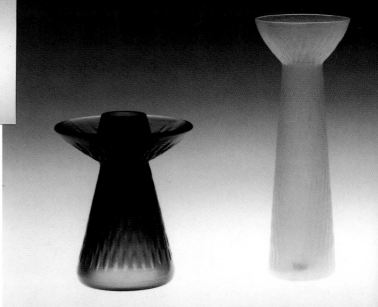

6.45 Left, green footed mayonnaise with crush ice finish, D. 6 1/2 in.; center, bowl with crushed ice finish on solid crystal foot; right, thick bowl found in the morgue, possibly an experimental piece. *Courtesy of the Huntington Musuem of Art*

6.46 Closer view of heavy bowl showing textural effect created by internal air pockets and bubbles. *Courtesy of the Huntington Museum of Art*

6.47 Top, Fostoria ebony plate with interior concentric circles and foot (not shown) with impressed diamond pattern, D. 7 1/8 in.; bottom, ebony bowl , D. 5 3/8 in., found in the morgue and probably Fostoria. *Courtesy of the Huntington Museum of Art*

6.48 Plate with abstract linear pattern on a frosted surface, found in morgue and possibly an experimental piece. *Courtesy of the Huntington Museum of Art*

6.49 No. 4161 Karnak from the Modern Primitive series of the early 1960s with pressed pattern resembling animal spots or stonework; although the appearance may be crude and heavy, these items are surprisingly thin-walled and delicate. Left, 6-oz. juice glass, H. 3 3/4in.; right, 12-oz. dessert bowl, D. 4 1/4 in. both in smoke and with etched mark at the base FOSTORIA.

6.50 Karnak juice tumblers and dessert bowls in amber, with paper labels and etched mark at the base FOSTORIA.

6.51 Detail of Karnak texture.

6.52 Karnak 21-oz. cooler, H. 6 3/4 in.; 14-oz. bevereage/water, H. 5 in.; and 6-oz. juice glasses, H. 3 3/4 in. in colors amber, smoke, pink, and crystal, each with etched mark FOSTORIA, some with paper label.

Labels

Fostoria plastic sign of brown logo

Brown label used 1924-1957

Fostoria plastic sign with red, white, and blue logo

Label used from 1957 on

Moon Mist

Late red, white, and blue label

Milk glass label

Milk glass label

Etched mark

Patterns and Decorations

The following chart is a list of about 1,000 names of patterns and decorations and their designated numbers. Two digit numbers (22-29, 60-76, etc.) indicate the time period during which an item was introduced according to Liebmann. Four digit dates (1909-28, 1922-30, etc.) indicate a production period or approximate dates of introduction and discontinuation, from Weatherman, Kerr, Long & Seate, and others. A single year (1888) indicates the approximate year of introduction, especially for very early items . The notation c61 or c82 means that it was in the 1961 or 1982 catalog. A date preceded by 'd' shows that it was discontinued in that year. The abbreviation 're' means that it was reissued at a later date, which can be after 1986 if Lancaster Colony is having the pattern made again. If sources disagree on dates, both versions are included. This lengthy, yet obviously incomplete, list is intended as a guide, to be revised as more information is found by researchers involved in this challenging task. *Use of catalog illustrations courtesy of Lancaster Colony*

American

American Beauty

American Lady

April Love

Argus

Arlington

Artisan

Aspen

Name	Number	Category	Years
Acanthus	282	plate etching	1930-33
Airdale	175	cutting	1924-28
Alaska	54	decoration	1925-31
Alexis	1630 line	pressed	1909-25
Allegro	672	decoration	1966-71
Allegro	748	cutting	1935-44
Aloha	805	cutting	1940-54
Alta	2863/924	cutting	1974-75
Ambassador	635, 637	decoration	1956-71
American	2056 line	pressed	1915-85; re
American Beauty	858	cutting	1958-63
American Lady	5056 line	blown	1933-73
American Milestones	555 or705	commemorative	1971-76
American Whitehall (American)		pressed	re
Amherst (Seville)	58	decoration	1926-34
Andover	665	decoration	1961-78
Anniversary	634	decoration	1954-75
Announcement	666	decoration	1964-84
Antique	56	decoration	20-29
Apple Blossom	516	decoration	30-42
Apple Blossom	138, 205	cutting	28-37; 1918-39; 1918-29
April Love	866	cutting	1957-59; c61
Arbor	184	cutting	1926-28
Arcady	326	plate etching	1936-55
Archer	24	carving	1940-44
Argu		pressed	1960s
Argus	2770 line	pressed	1960-85; re
Ariel	93	crystal tracing	1940-44
Aristocrat	2843	pressed	1970s
Arlington	2684 line	pressed	c61
Arlington	70	decoration	20-29
Arrow	142, 205	cutting	1919-25
Artichoke (also Frosted)	205	pressed	1890
Artisan	2570-2703 line	pressed	1961-64
Arvida	185	cutting	1927-28
Aspen	2861 line	pressed	1974-83
Astrid	6030 line	blown	1942-78
Athenian	770	cutting	1937-44; c61
Athens	AT 01	cutting	76-86
Atlanta	500	pressed	1895
Aura	AU 02	cutting	76-86
Aurora	651	decoration	1954-82
Autumn	850	cutting	1957-59; c61
Avalon	832	cutting	1952-55; c61
Avalon	85	needle etching	1929-31
Aztec	6	carving	1938-42
Ballerina	900	cutting	1964-68
Ballet	91	needle etching	1935-44
Ballet	828	cutting	1952-66
Bands	4	carving	37-60
Banner	45	carving	1941-44
Banquet	342	plate etching	37-60
Barcelona	705	cutting	28-37
Barcelona	27	crystal print	1971-74
Baroness		blown	76-86
Baronet	847	cutting	1936-44; 1956-66

Athenian

Autumn

Avalon

Ballet

Baronet

Baroque

Beacon

Bedford

Betsy Ross

Bouquet

Bracelet

Brazilian

Bridal Belle

Bridal Crown

Bridal Wreath

Brighton

Name	Number	Technique	Date
Baronet	92	needle etching	1926-44
Baroque	2484 & 2496 line	pressed	1936-66
Beacon	767	cutting	1937-55; c61
Beacon Hill	917	cutting	1968-71
Beaded Flange		pressed	1891
Bedford	1000	pressed	1901-04
Bellweather	BE 05	cutting	76-86
Beloved	647	decoration	1960-82
Bennington	BE 04	pressed	1983-86
Berkeley	909	cutting	1966-68
Berkshire	6105 line	blown	1966-74
Berry	2712 line	pressed	37-60; 1961-65
Berry	188	cutting	1928-29
Betrothal	673	decoration	1966-71
Betsy Ross (Wistar)	2620 line	pressed	1961-65
Beverly	276	plate etching	1927-34
Bianca	22	crystal print	1969-71
Billow	118	cutting	1913-18
Bird Pattern	22	carving	37-60
Biscayne	6122 line	blown	1970-74
Black and Gold	23	decoration	20-29
Blackberry	205	etching	1908-10
Black Border	20	decoration	1920s
Block	38 1/2	needle etching	1904-13; 1915-28
Blue and Gold	22	decoration	20-29
Blue Bird	16	decoration	1910-19
Blue Border	19	decoration	1920s
Blue Meadow	8	crystal	37-60
Bordeaux	758	cutting	1936-44
Bouquet	342	plate etching	1949-61
Bouquet	756	cutting	1935-39
Bracelet	694	decoration	1976-83
Bracelet	838	cutting	1953-57; c61; c82
Brazilian	600	pressed	1898-1913
Bridal Belle	639, 955	decoration	1957-74
Bridal Crown	882	cutting	1961-66
Bridal Shower	897	cutting	1963-71
Bridal Shower	768	cutting	1937-39
Bridal Wreath	833	cutting	1952-66
Bridesmaid	658	decoration	1962-71
Brighton	801	cutting	1940-55; c61
Brilliant	1001	pressed	1901-04
Brilliant	1871	pressed	1914-20
Bristol	880	cutting	1960-63
Bristol	710	cutting	1933-39
Brocade	674	decoration	1966-71
Brocade	13	carving	1939-44
Brocade	291	etching	1930-42
Brocade	30	crystal print	1971-74
Brunswick	79	needle etching	1926-33
Brunswick	198	cutting	22-29
Bubble Baby	28	carving	1940-44
Bubble Balls	4116, 4126	blown	1930s
Buckingham	721	cutting	1933-35
Burgundy	878	cutting	1960-69
Burnished Gold Highlight	632	decoration	37-60
Buttercup	340	plate etching	1941-60; c61; c82
Butterfly	508	decoration	28-37
Cabot	6025 line	blown	1939-58
Cadence	806	cutting	1940-44
Camden	84	needle etching	1928-31
Camelia	344	plate etching	1952-66
Camelot	6009 line	blown	1933-41; re 1979-80
Cameo	88	needle etching	1934-40

Brilliant

Bristol

Burgundy

Buttercup

Camelia

Cameo

Carousel

Cascade

Cathedral

Chapel Bells

Chatham

Chintz

Chippendale

Christiana

Circlet

Coin Glass

Colonial Mirror

Name	Number	Type	Years
Cameo	28	crystal print	1971-83
Cameo Ware	604	pressed	1898
Candlelight	652	decoration	1961-72; 1968-73
Cantata	907	cutting	1965-71
Canterbury	716	cutting	1933-36
Capri	6045 line	blown	1952-65
Captain Kidd (Virginia)	150	pressed	1888
Captiva	CA 16	pressed	1983-86
Caribbean	6112 line	decoration	
Caribbean	2808 line	blown	1969-75
Carillon	915	cutting	1967-69
Carlisle	715	cutting	1933-36
Carmel		blown	76-86
Carmen	575	carving	1898
Carnival	7	carving	1938-42
Carousel	863	cutting	1958-76; c82
Cascade	112	pressed	1888
Cascade	8	decoration	1920s
Cascade	636	decoration	1956-66; 1961-70
Castle	87	needle etching	1933-40
Casual Flair	4180 line	blown	1958-62
Catalina	6046 line	blown	1951-55
Cathedral	792	cutting	1939-44; c61
Cattails	145	cutting	1920s
Cavendish	754	cutting	1935-40
Celebration	698	decoration	60-76; 1980-85
Celebration	CE 03	blown	c82
Celebrity	6106 line	blown	1966-71
Celebrity	749	cutting	1935-44
Celeste	6072 line	blown	1957-74
Celestial	731	cutting	1934-38
Celestial		blown	76-86
Cellini	6024 line	blown	1940-75
Century	2630 line	pressed	1949-85
Chain Design	42	needle etching	1898-1928
Chalice	6059 line	blown	1955-65
Chalice	6029 line	blown	1941-44
Chalice	812	cutting	1941-44
Chanticleer	41	carving	1940-44
Chapel Bells	888	cutting	1961-75; c82
Chateau	6087 line	blown	1959-70
Chateau	315	plate etching	1933-40
Chatham	829	cutting	1952-61
Chatteres	197	cutting	1929-31
Chelsea	783	cutting	1938-44
Cherish	681	decoration	1969-83
Chintz	338	plate etching	1940-82+
Chippendale	CH05	plate etching	1983-86
Chippendale	788	cutting	1939-44; c61
Christiana	814	cutting	1942-70; c82
Christine	798	cutting	1940-44
Christmas Bells		cut & decorated	76-86
Chrysanthemum	133	cutting	1918-29
Chrysanthemum		deep etching	1921-24
Circlet	840	cutting	1954-70
Classic	6011 line	blown	37-60; 1934-64
Classic Gold	641	decoration	1958-83
Clover	132	cutting	1918-29
Club	603, 604, 611, 612	decoration	1931-33
Cockatoo	505	decoration	30-37
Coin Glass	1372 line	pressed	1958-82; re
Coin Gold	1, 2, 6, 7, 15	decoration	1906-1920s
Colfax	6023 line	blown	1940-76
Colonial	5	carving	1938-42
Colonial	2222 line	pressed	1920s; re
Colonial Dame	5412 line	blown	1948-82
Colonial Mirror	334	plate etching	1939-45; c61
Colonial Prism	2183 line	pressed	1918-28
Colonial Prism	CO 13	pressed giftware	1978-83
Colony (Queen Anne)	2412 line	pressed	1938-79
Colorado	677	pressed	1888
Comet	702	cutting	1930-43
Congo	4162 line	pressed	1960s; 1955-65
Continental	6052 1/2 line	blown	1956-73
Contour	2638 line	pressed	1955-77

Congo

Contour

Corsage

Crest

Crown Collection

Cynthia

Cyrene

Debutante

Devon

Diamond Mirror

Diamond Sunburst

Contour	2666 line	pressed	1955-77
Contour	6060 line	blown	1955-77
Contrast	6120 line	blown	60-76
Contrast	6030 line	blown	1970s
Coral Pearl	623	decoration	1940-61
Cordelia	82	needle etching	1927-31
Cornucopia	46	carving	1941-44
Coronada (Royal)	49	decoration	1925-34
Coronet	656	decoration	1962-71
Coronet	2560 line	pressed	1938-60
Corsage	325	plate etching	1935-60
Corsage Plum	6126 line	blown	1973-78
Cotillion	892	cutting	1962-71
Countess		blown	76-86
Country Garden	13	crystal	37-60
Courtship	6051 1/2 line	blown	1956-78+
Coventry	2796 line	pressed	60-76
Coventry	2834 line	pressed	1960s-73
Coventry	807	cutting	1940-44
Craquelled		decoration	1910-20
Cresap	1497 reissue	pressed	1969
Crest	843	cutting	1955-63
Crimson Rose	3	decoration	1910-19
Criterion	65	decoration	20-29
Crossed Shields	1303	pressed	1905
Crown Collection	2749-51 line	pressed	1950s-65
Crystal Twist	6101 line	blown	1962-71
Crystal Wedding	1460 line	pressed	1906-08
Cumberland	762	cutting	1936-40
Cupid	288	plate etching	1927-29
Cynthia	785	cutting	1938-66
Cynthia	170	cutting	1924-28
Cyrene	763	cutting	1936-44; c61
Czarina	444	pressed	1890s
Daffodil		deep etching	1921-24
Daisy	17	decoration	1920s
Daisy	324	plate etching	1935-44
Daisy and Button	2710 line	pressed	1950s-65
Daisy and Fern		deep etching	1921-24
Daphne	797	cutting	1939-44
Dawn	2670 line	pressed	1953-66
Debutante	6100 line	blown	1962-85
Decorator	2691 line	pressed	1956-60
Deer	A,B,C,D	cuttings	30-42
Delphian	272	plate etching	1925-28
Delphine	199	cutting	1931
Devon	876	cutting	1960-63
Diadem	6056 line	blown	1954-65
Diadem	2430 line	pressed	1929-44
Diamond Mirror		pressed	pre-1900
Diamond Sunburst	2711 line	pressed	1960s
Diana	601	pressed	1898-1901 or 13
Directoire	736	cutting	1934-40; c61
Distinction	6125 line	blown	1972-85
Dog Show	49	carving	37-60
Dolly Madison	786	cutting	1939-72+
Dolphin	27	carving	1940-44
Doncaster	718	cutting	1933-44
Drape	784	cutting	1938-44; c61
Drape	1300 line	pressed	1904-06; re 1969
Dresden	12	decoration	1910-19
Drum	781	cutting	1938-44
DuBarry	48	decoration	20-29
Duchess	853	cutting	1957-59; c61
Duchess (Delphian)	51	decoration	1925-28
Dusk	2671 line	pressed	1953-65
Eaton	713	cutting	1933-39

Diana

Directoire

Distinction

Dolly Madison

Drape

Duchess

Dusk

Edgewood

Embrace

Empress

Encore

Evening Star

Fairlane

Fairmont

Fantasy

Festival

Festoon

Foster Block (Virginia)

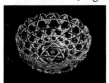

Fostoria Swirl

Fostoria Wheat

Name	Number	Technique	Dates
Edgewood	675	pressed	1898-1908
Eilene	83	needle etching	1928-33
Elegance	6064 1/2 line	blown	1956-71
Elephant	36	carving	1940-44
Eloquence	6120 line	blown	1971-78
Eloquence (Gold)	686	decoration	1970-75
Eloquence (Platinum)	687	decoration	1970-79
Eloquence Venice	688	decoration	
Elsinore	89	needle etching	1934-40
Embassy	728	cutting	1933-38
Embassy	6083 line	blown	1959-74
Embrace	887	cutting	1961-66
Empire	238	plate etching	1915-1928
Empire	908	cutting	1966-70
Empress	861	cutting	1958-71
Empress	29	decoration	1924-30
Enamel	17, 19, & 20	decoration	20-29
Enamel and Gold	21	decoration	20-29
Enchantment	6074 line	blown	1958-65
Encore	860	cutting	1958-60; c61
Encrusted Gold	35 & 45	decoration	20-29
Engagement	648	decoration	1960-65;1960-82
Envoy	6027 line	blown	1940-57
Ermine	602	pressed	1898
Essex	1372 line	pressed	1905-25
Eton	713	cutting	1932-39
Evangeline	752	cutting	1935-39
Evening Breeze	891	cutting	1962-66
Evening Star	869	cutting	37-60; c61
Exeter	6109 line	blown	1967-71
Facet	2762 line	pressed	60-76
Fairfax	2375 line	pressed	1927-60
Fairfax	167, 205	cutting	1922-29
Fairlane	2916 line	pressed	1976-83
Fairmont	2718 line	pressed	1958-65
Fantasy	17	crystal print	1959-66
Fantasy	747	cutting	1936-38
Fascination	6080 line	blown	1958-85
Federal	771	cutting	1937-44
Fern	305	plate etching	1929-34
Fern	501	decoration	1929-34
Festival	45	plate etching	1981-83
Festival	FE 04	blown	76-86
Festive	6127 line	blown	1975-83
Festoon	738	cutting	1934-40; c61
Fifth Avenue	114	needle etching	pre-1900-21
Firelight	657	decoration	1963-85
Firenze (Verona)	281	plate etching	1931-32
First Love	918	cutting	1968-71
Flame	2545 line	pressed	1936-44
Flat Diamond Box	301		
Flemish	1913 line	pressed	1913-28; re 69
Flemish	319	plate etching	1933-39
Fleur-de-lis	172-178	cutting	1925-28
Fleurette	26	crystal print	1972-75
Florentine	311	plate etching	1931-44
Florid	256	plate etching	1920-28
Florin	619	decoration	1940-44
Flower Girl	659	decoration	1962-68
Flower Song	894	cutting	60-76
Forever	904	cutting	1964-66
Forget-me-not	147	cutting	1920s
Formal Garden	700	cutting	1930-31
Formality	818	cutting	1942-52
Foster Block (Virginia)	140	pressed	1888
Fostoria Prism	1917	cutting	1917
Fostoria Ruby		pressed	pre-1892
Fostoria Swirl	175	pressed	1890
Fostoria Wheat	837	cutting	1953-74
Fountain	901	cutting	1964-66
Fountain	307	plate etching	1929-31

Frosted Artichoke

Gadroon

Garland

Gazebo

Georgian

Gold Coin

Golden Lace

Golden Love

Gossamer

Grand Majesty

Fresno	78	needle etching	1925-31
Frisco	1229 line	pressed	1898-1904; re, c69
Frosted Artichoke	205	pressed	pre-1891
Frosted Stem	6011 line	blown	1930s
Fruit	320	plate etching	1933-39
Fruit and Flowers	523	decoration	37-60
Fuchsia	310	plate etching	1931-44
Gadroon	816	cutting	1947-57; c61
Gala	6147 line	blown	1981-85
Garden Center	2640 line		
Garland	237	plate etching	1915-29
Garland	205	etching	
Garland	859	cutting	1958-60; c61
Garter	44	needle etching	1898-1928
Gas Lights		pressed	76-86
Gazebo	6126 line	blown	60-76; 1980-85
Geneva	135	cutting	1918-28
Georgetown	906	cutting	1965-74
Georgian	885	cutting	1961-83
Georgian	791	cutting	1939-44
Giftware	2470	pressed	1933-44
Glacier	2510 line	pressed	1935-44
Glamour	6103 line	blown	1964-83
Glendale	919	cutting	1967-73
Gloucester	898	cutting	1963-70
Gold Coin	646	decoration on 1372	1960-70
Gold Decoration	634	decoration	37-60
Gold Decoration	669	decoration	60-76
Gold (Italian) Lace	514	decoration	1938-44
Golden Belle	677	decoration	1968-70s
Golden Flair	643	decoration	1959-70s
Golden Garland	664	decoration	1964-68
Golden Grail	644	decoration	1959-74
Golden Lace	645	decoration	1959-76
Golden Love	640	decoration	1958-66
Golden Song	662	decoration	37-60; 1964-69
Golden Swirl	614	decoration	1935-38
Golden Triumph	6112 line	blown	1969-73
Golden Twilight	12	crystal	37-60
Goldwood	50	decoration	1922-29
Gossamer	852	cutting	1957-63
Gossamer	746	cutting	1935-40
Gothic	774	cutting	1938-44
Gourmet	2785 line	pressed	76-86; 1965-70
Granada	923	cutting	1971-74
Grand Majesty	GR 03, 38	plate etching	1979-81
Grape	287	plate etching	1927-30
Grape	517	decoration	28-37
Grape Leaf	2513 line	pressed	1935-42
Grape Stem	61-64	decoration	1920s
Greek Design	45	needle etching	1898-1928
Greek Figure		deep etching	1921-24
Greek Key	819	cutting	1942-44
Greenbrier	6026 line	blown	1940-76
Greenbrier	14	crystal	37-60
Greenfield	935	cutting	1976-83
Greenfield	916	cutting	1967-69
Grenada	923	cutting	60-76
Greyhounds	25	carving	1940-44
Grille	236	plate etching	1915-25
Gros Point	43	carving	1940-44
Halo	689	decoration	1970-74
Hammered Silver	66	decoration	20-29
Hartford	501	pressed	1898-1901
Harvest	6097 line	blown	60-76; c82
Hawaiian	2737 line	pressed	1961-64
Hawthorne	790	cutting	1939-44
Heather	343	plate etching	1949-72

Greenfield

Harvest

Hawaiian

Heather

Heirloom

Heraldry

Heritage

Holly

Homespun

Inca

Ingrid

Ivy

Jenny Lind

Juliet

June

Karnak

Kimberly

Lacy Leaf

Late Icicle

Name	Number	Type	Date
Heavy Jewel	1225	pressed	1900
Heirloom	36	plate etching	1976-83
Heirloom	751	cutting	1935-39
Heirloom	5056 line	pressed	1959-70
Henry Ford Museum	2776-2790	pressed	1963-70
Heraldry	743	cutting	1935-44; c61
Heritage	849	cutting	1956-59; c61
Heritage	2887 line	pressed	1970s-85-
Hermitage	2449 line	pressed	1932-45
Heron	31	carving	1941-44
Highlight	HI 01	pressed	76-86
Highlighted Blue Spray	631	decoration	37-60
Holiday	2643	pressed	1949-60
Holly	815	cutting	1941-72+
Hollyhocks	16	carving	1940-44
Homespun	4183 line	blown	1959-65
Horizon	2650 line	tumblers	1952-55
Horizon	5650 line	blown	1951-58
Horse	35	carving	1940-44
Humpty Dumpty	4146	blown	37-60
Hunt	34	carving	1940-44
I. C.	1819 line	pressed	1911-15
Icicle	IC	blown	76-86; c82
Icicle	59	carving	1982
Illusion	6111 line	blown	1969-85
Images	IM 02	pressed	76-86
Imperial	47	decoration	20-29
Impressions	IM 01	pressed	76-86
Inca	4163 line	pressed	1960s; 1955-65
Ingrid	794	cutting	1939-44
Ingrid	836	cutting	1953-71
Inspiration	6107	blown	1966-70s
Interpretations	IN 03	pressed	76-86
Intimate	31	crystal print	1971-74
Inverness	711	cutting	1933-36
Invitation	660	decoration	1963-83
Irish Lace	36 & 37	needle etching	1898-1927
Italian (Gold)Lace	514	decoration	1938-44
Ivy	205, 235	plate etching	1913-18
Ivy	745	cutting	1935-44; c61
Jamestown	2719 line	pressed	1958-85
Jefferson	6104 line	blown	1964-73
Jenny Lind	824-835	pressed	1955-65
Jubilee	699	decoration	60-76;1981-83
Jubilee	699 line	blown	1982-
Juliet	865	cutting	1959-70
June	279	plate etching	1928-52
Juniper	JU 05	pressed	1983-86
Karnak	4161 line	pressed	1955-65; 1961-65
Kashmir	283	plate etching	1930-34
Kenmore	176, 176 1/2	cutting	1925-28
Kent	2424 line	pressed	1939-44
Kent	6079 line	blown	1958-71
Kimberly	775	cutting	1938-44
Kimberly	855	cutting	1957-66
Kimberly	2990 line	pressed	1979-86
King George	11	carving	37-60
Kingsley	192	cutting	1929-30
Kingston (Camden)	41	decoration	1929-31
Kismet	10	crystal	37-60
Kornflower	234	plate etching	1913-18
Lace Works	201	etching	1904-10
Lacy Leaf	6	crystal print	37-60; c61
Lafayette	2440 line	pressed	1931-60
Lamp Base Stars	23B	carving	37-60
Lancaster	719	cutting	1933-36
Landscape		deep etching	1921-24
Large Cloverleaf	47	needle etching	pre-1900-1920
Large Sunburst Star	81	cutting	1904-29
Late Icicle	162	pressed	1889

Laurel

Lenox

Lido

Living Rose

Lotus

Lynwood

Mardi Gras

Marquise

Maytime

Meadow Rose

Melba

Melody

Lattice	196	cutting	1929
Laurel	31	decoration	1924-30
Laurel	776	cutting	1938-60
Laurel Band	20	carving	37-60
Legacy	635	decoration	1956-71
Legion	309	plate etching	1931-40
Leicester	722 1/2	cutting	1933-35
Lenore	73	needle etchlng	1923-31
Lenox	330	plate etching	1937-44
Lexington	2449 line	pressed	1974-79
Liana Gold	LI 05	cutting	76-86
Liana Platinum	LI 04	cutting	76-86
Lido	329	plate etching	1937-55; c61
Lily-of-the-Valley	19	carving	1940-44
Lily-of-the-Valley	241	plate etching	1915-28
Lincoln	1861 line	pressed	1912-28
Lineal	899	cutting	1963-66
Living Rose	5	crystal print	1956-59; c61
Long Buttress	1299	pressed	1904-13
Lorraine	301	pressed	1891
Lotus	6144 line	blown	1980-85
Lotus	232	plate etching	1913-28
Louis XVI		deep etching	1921-24
Louisa	168	cutting	1922-28
Louise	1121	pressed	1902-07 re 69
Lovelight	671	decoration	1966-71+
Love Song	655	decoration	1961-74
Lucere	1515 line	pressed	1907-15
Lucerne	778	cutting	1938-39
Lynn	180	cutting	1925-28
Lynwood	4	crystal print	1956-65
Lyre	30	carving	1940-44
Lyric	796	cutting	1939-44
Lyric	6061 line	blown	1955-65
M.G.	2675	pressed	37-60
Mademoiselle	6033 line	blown	1949-75
Manhattan	725	cutting	1933-39
Manor	286	plate etching	1931-44
Mantilla	675	decoration	1966-71
Mardi Gras	627	decoration	37-60
Mardi Gras	765	cutting	1937-44; c61
Marguerite	240	pressed	1888
Marilyn	6055 line	blown	1954-77
Marine Scene		deep etching	1921-24
Marlboro	717	cutting	1933-39
Marquette	733	cutting	1934-36
Marquiol	831	cutting	37-60
Marquise	692	decoration	1971-75
Marquise	831	cutting	1952-55; c61
Matrimony	910	cutting	1966-70s
Mayday	312	plate etching	1931
Mayfair	2419 line	pressed	1930-44
Mayflower	332	plate etching	1939-55
Maypole	6149 line	blown	1982
Maypole (Colony)	6149 line	pressed	1982
Maytime	845	cutting	1956-59; c61
Meadow Rose	328	plate etching	1937-72+
Melamine		plastic	60-76
Melba	761	cutting	1936-44; c61
Melody	6020 line	blown	1938-58
Melody	881	cutting	1960-66
Melrose	268	plate etching	1924-29
Memories	750	cutting	1935-36
Mesa	605?	blown	1960s
Mesa	4186 line	pressed	1968-76
Meteor	726	cutting	1933-39
Miami	42	decoration	1924-30
Midnight Rose	316	plate etching	1933-57
Milady	895	cutting	1963-66
Milkweed	7	crystal print	37-60
Millefleur	195	cutting	1929-40
Minuet	826	cutting	1950-60
Minuet	285	plate etchlng	1930-34
Mission	116	cutting	1913-29
Miscellaneous	38	carving	37-60
Misty	6129 line	blown	1978-83
Misty Platinum	695	decoration	1978-82

Monarch

Monroe

Monticello

Moonbeam

Moonstone

Mulberry

Navarre

Nosegay

Nouveau

Nova

Name	Line	Type	Dates
Modern Vintage	255	plate etching	1920-29
Module	2824 line	pressed	1971-74
Monarch	2903 line	pressed	76-86
Monarch	60	decoration	1926-29
Monarch	2903 line	blown	76-86
Monarch	MO 11, 2903	pressed	1970s-85
Monet	MO 12	pressed	1980-85; re
Monroe	86	needle etching	1933-40
Monroe	2694 line	pressed	1950s-65
Monroe	2678 line	pressed	c61
Monte Carlo	912	cutting	1967-71
Monticello	886	cutting	1961-71
Moonbeam	856	cutting	1957-66
Moonglow	649	decoration	1960-68
Moon Mist	684	decoration	1969-73
Moonring	6052, 4132 line	blown	1953-65
Moonstone	2882 line	pressed	1974-82; re
Morgantown	7780 line	blown	60-76
Morning Glory	12	carving	1939-44
Morning Glory	313	plate etching	1931-44
Mother of Pearl	622	decoration	c61
Mt. Vernon	817	cutting	1942-55
Mulberry	799	cutting	1940-60; c61
Myriad	2592 line	pressed	1941-45
Mystic	270, 270 1/2	plate etching	1924-29
Nairn	708	cutting	1933-44
Narcissus	17	carving	37-60
National	727	cutting	1933-44
Navarre	327	plate etching	1936-83
Nectar	322	plate etching	1934-43
Needlepoint	4184 line	blown	1959-65
Neo Classic	6011 line	blown	1934-41; 1949-65
New Adam	252	plate etching	1918-28
New Garland	284	plate etching	1930-34
Newport	9	decoration	1924-30
New Vintage	227	plate etching	1913-28
New Yorker	703	cutting	1930-44
Niagara	793	pressed	1900-01
Niagara	6026/2 line	blown	1940-65
Nightmare	621	decoration	1940-44
Nightmare	39	carving	1940-44
Nine Stars	23	carving	37-60
19th Hole	15	carving	1940-44
Nome	40	decoration	1924-30
Nordic	892	blown	1939-44
Nordic	6077 line	blown	1958-65
Northampton	720	cutting	76-86
Nosegay	834	cutting	1953-73
Nottingham	720	cutting	1933-35
Nouveau	42	plate etching	1980-83
Nova	934	cutting	1976-82
Nugget	507	decoration	28-37
Nuptial	21	crystal print	1969-75
Oak Leaf	290	plate etching	1928-31
Oakwood	72	decoration	1928-31
Old English	1460 line	pressed	1906-08
Old Williamsburg		pressed	76-86
Olive	235	pressed	1888
Olympic Gold	680	decoration	1968-71
Olympic Platinum	679	decoration	1968-71
Orange Blossom		deep etching	1920-24
Orange Blossom	911	cutting	1966-68
Orbit	742	cutting	1934-38
Orchid	48	carving	1941-43
Orient	265	plate etching	1922-28
Oriental	250	etching	1918-29
Oriental		deep etching	1921-24
Orleans	194	cutting	1929-30
Orleans	6089 line	blown	1960-77
Overture	867	cutting	1959-61
Oxford	714	cutting	1933-44
Pagoda	90	needle etching	1935-44
Palm Leaf	73	decoration	1930-42
Palmetto	755	cutting	1935-44
Panelled Diamond Point	2860 line	pressed	1973-75
	795	cutting	1939-44

Overture

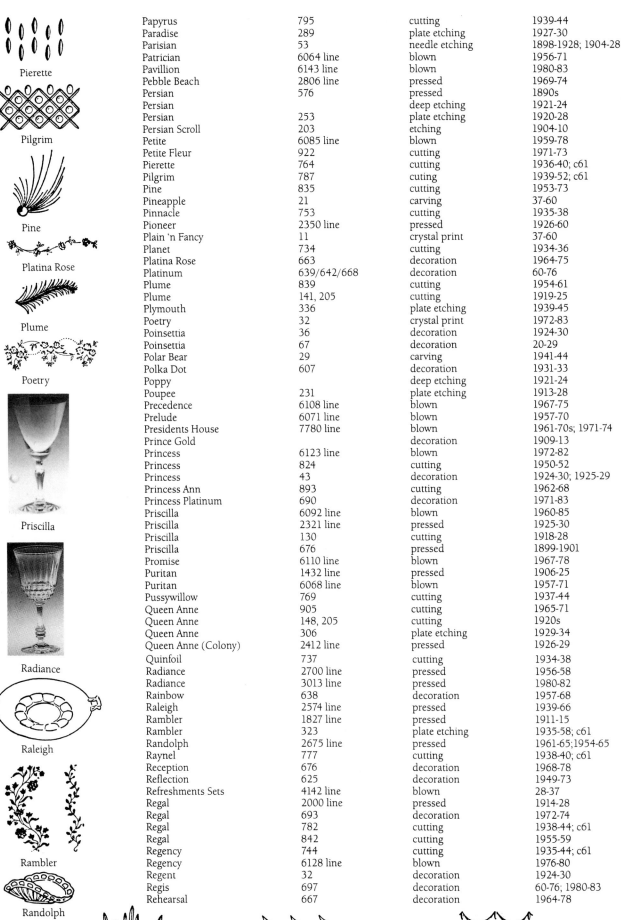

Name	Number	Type	Dates
Papyrus	795	cutting	1939-44
Paradise	289	plate etching	1927-30
Parisian	53	needle etching	1898-1928; 1904-28
Patrician	6064 line	blown	1956-71
Pavillion	6143 line	blown	1980-83
Pebble Beach	2806 line	pressed	1969-74
Persian	576	pressed	1890s
Persian		deep etching	1921-24
Persian	253	plate etching	1920-28
Persian Scroll	203	etching	1904-10
Petite	6085 line	blown	1959-78
Petite Fleur	922	cutting	1971-73
Pierette	764	cutting	1936-40; c61
Pilgrim	787	cuting	1939-52; c61
Pine	835	cutting	1953-73
Pineapple	21	carving	37-60
Pinnacle	753	cutting	1935-38
Pioneer	2350 line	pressed	1926-60
Plain 'n Fancy	11	crystal print	37-60
Planet	734	cutting	1934-36
Platina Rose	663	decoration	1964-75
Platinum	639/642/668	decoration	60-76
Plume	839	cutting	1954-61
Plume	141, 205	cutting	1919-25
Plymouth	336	plate etching	1939-45
Poetry	32	crystal print	1972-83
Poinsettia	36	decoration	1924-30
Poinsettia	67	decoration	20-29
Polar Bear	29	carving	1941-44
Polka Dot	607	decoration	1931-33
Poppy		deep etching	1921-24
Poupee	231	plate etching	1913-28
Precedence	6108 line	blown	1967-75
Prelude	6071 line	blown	1957-70
Presidents House	7780 line	blown	1961-70s; 1971-74
Prince Gold		decoration	1909-13
Princess	6123 line	blown	1972-82
Princess	824	cutting	1950-52
Princess	43	decoration	1924-30; 1925-29
Princess Ann	893	cutting	1962-68
Princess Platinum	690	decoration	1971-83
Priscilla	6092 line	blown	1960-85
Priscilla	2321 line	pressed	1925-30
Priscilla	130	cutting	1918-28
Priscilla	676	pressed	1899-1901
Promise	6110 line	blown	1967-78
Puritan	1432 line	pressed	1906-25
Puritan	6068 line	blown	1957-71
Pussywillow	769	cutting	1937-44
Queen Anne	905	cutting	1965-71
Queen Anne	148, 205	cutting	1920s
Queen Anne	306	plate etching	1929-34
Queen Anne (Colony)	2412 line	pressed	1926-29
Quinfoil	737	cutting	1934-38
Radiance	2700 line	pressed	1956-58
Radiance	3013 line	pressed	1980-82
Rainbow	638	decoration	1957-68
Raleigh	2574 line	pressed	1939-66
Rambler	1827 line	pressed	1911-15
Rambler	323	plate etching	1935-58; c61
Randolph	2675 line	pressed	1961-65;1954-65
Raynel	777	cutting	1938-40; c61
Reception	676	decoration	1968-78
Reflection	625	decoration	1949-73
Refreshments Sets	4142 line	blown	28-37
Regal	2000 line	pressed	1914-28
Regal	693	decoration	1972-74
Regal	782	cutting	1938-44; c61
Regal	842	cutting	1955-59
Regency	744	cutting	1935-44; c61
Regency	6128 line	blown	1976-80
Regent	32	decoration	1924-30
Regis	697	decoration	60-76; 1980-83
Rehearsal	667	decoration	1964-78

Pierette

Pilgrim

Pine

Platina Rose

Plume

Poetry

Priscilla

Radiance

Raleigh

Rambler

Randolph

Raynel

Regal

Regency

Revere

Rheims

Ripple

Robin Hood

Rocket

Rock Garden

Romance

Rondo

Rose

Rosette

Name	Number	Type	Dates
Remembrance	670	decoration	1966-71
Renaissance Gold	678	decoration	1968-83
Renaissance Platinum	682	decoration	1969-83
Revere	825	cutting	1950-61; c61
Rhapsody	6055 1/2 line	blown	1955-75
Rheims	803	cutting	1940-44; c61
Rhythm	773	cutting	1938-43
Rhythmic	191	cutting	22-29
Richelieu	515	decoration	1938-40
Richmond	654	decoration	1960-85
Richmond	74	needle etching	1924-42
Ringlet	95	crystal tracing	1940-44
Ringlet	6051 line	blown	1953-66
Ring o' Roses	9	crystal print	37-60
Ripple	766	cutting	1937-44; c61
Rivera	44	decoration	1924-30
Robin Hood	603	pressed	1898-1903
Rock Crystal	4	cutting	1903-15
Rock Crystal	6000-6009 line	blown	1933-44
Rocket	729	cutting	1934-44; c61
Rock Garden	739	cutting	1934-44; c61
Rococo	234	pressed	1891
Rogene	269	plate etching	1924-28
Romance	341	plate etching	1942-72+
Rondeau	740	cutting	1934-36
Rondel	6019 line	blown	1937-44
Rondo	830	cutting	1952-55; c61
Rooster	37	carving	1940-47
Rosalie	19	crystal print	1963-76
Rosby	1704 line	pressed	1910-28 +some
Rose	827	cutting	1951-74
Rose	144	cutting	1920s
Rose and Blue	5	decoration	1910-19
Rose and Gold	11	decoration	1910-19
Rosedale	25	engraving	1924-29
Rosemary	339	plate etching	1940-44
Rosette	3	crystal print	1956; c61
Rosette	2501 line	intaglio	1936-44
Rosilyn	249	plate etching	1918-28
Roulette	2739	blown	1968
Royal	39	decoration	1924-30
Royal	273	plate etching	1925-32; 1925-38
Royal Garden	704	cutting	28-37
Ruby		stained decoration	1891
Ruth	233	pressed	1891
Rutledge	6036 line	blown	1951-77
St. Bernard	450	pressed	early 1890s
St. Regis	873	cutting	1959-61
St. Regis	616	decoration	1939-44
Salon	804	cutting	1940-44
Sampler	337	plate etching	1939-44
San Francisco		blown	76-86
Satin Ribbons	SA 05	plate etching	1983-86
Saturn	69	decoration	20-29
Saturn	605	decoration	1931-33
Savannah	902	cutting	1964-69
Saybrooke	813	cutting	1941-44
Sceptre	6017 line	blown	1938-76
Scotch Plaid	38	needle etching	pre-1898-1915
Sculpture	2740-2745 line	pressed	1961-70
Seascape	2685 line	pressed	1954-58
Sea Shells	2825, 2844 line	pressed	1971-73
Seaweed	732	cutting	1934-36
Selma	800	cutting	1940-44; c61
Sentimental	25	crystal print	1971-76
Serenade	780	cutting	1938-44
Serenade	864	cutting	1959-66
Serendipity	2842 line	pressed	1970s
Serenity	35	plate etching	1975-83
Serenity	868	cutting	1957-66

St. Regis

Sculpture

Selma

Serenade

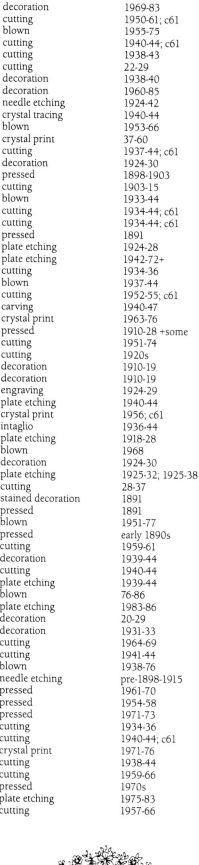

Serenity

Serenity

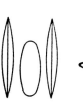

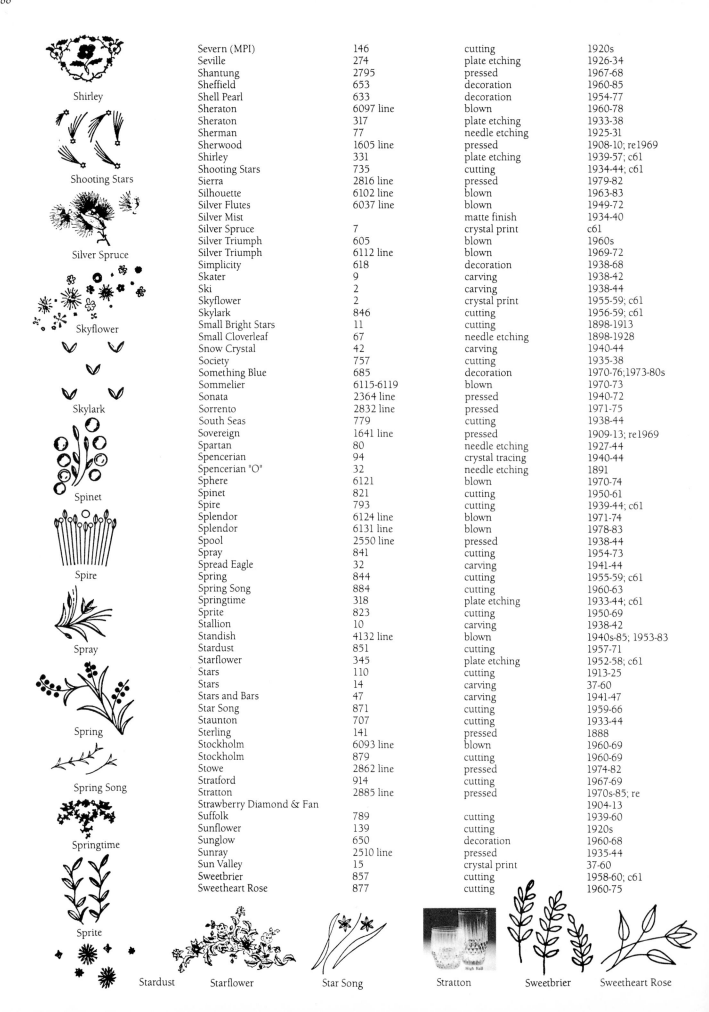

Name	Line/No.	Technique	Dates
Severn (MPI)	146	cutting	1920s
Seville	274	plate etching	1926-34
Shantung	2795	pressed	1967-68
Sheffield	653	decoration	1960-85
Shell Pearl	633	decoration	1954-77
Sheraton	6097 line	blown	1960-78
Sheraton	317	plate etching	1933-38
Sherman	77	needle etching	1925-31
Sherwood	1605 line	pressed	1908-10; re1969
Shirley	331	plate etching	1939-57; c61
Shooting Stars	735	cutting	1934-44; c61
Sierra	2816 line	pressed	1979-82
Silhouette	6102 line	blown	1963-83
Silver Flutes	6037 line	blown	1949-72
Silver Mist		matte finish	1934-40
Silver Spruce	7	crystal print	c61
Silver Triumph	605	blown	1960s
Silver Triumph	6112 line	blown	1969-72
Simplicity	618	decoration	1938-68
Skater	9	carving	1938-42
Ski	2	carving	1938-44
Skyflower	2	crystal print	1955-59; c61
Skylark	846	cutting	1956-59; c61
Small Bright Stars	11	cutting	1898-1913
Small Cloverleaf	67	needle etching	1898-1928
Snow Crystal	42	carving	1940-44
Society	757	cutting	1935-38
Something Blue	685	decoration	1970-76;1973-80s
Sommelier	6115-6119	blown	1970-73
Sonata	2364 line	pressed	1940-72
Sorrento	2832 line	pressed	1971-75
South Seas	779	cutting	1938-44
Sovereign	1641 line	pressed	1909-13; re1969
Spartan	80	needle etching	1927-44
Spencerian	94	crystal tracing	1940-44
Spencerian "O"	32	needle etching	1891
Sphere	6121	blown	1970-74
Spinet	821	cutting	1950-61
Spire	793	cutting	1939-44; c61
Splendor	6124 line	blown	1971-74
Splendor	6131 line	blown	1978-83
Spool	2550 line	pressed	1938-44
Spray	841	cutting	1954-73
Spread Eagle	32	carving	1941-44
Spring	844	cutting	1955-59; c61
Spring Song	884	cutting	1960-63
Springtime	318	plate etching	1933-44; c61
Sprite	823	cutting	1950-69
Stallion	10	carving	1938-42
Standish	4132 line	blown	1940s-85; 1953-83
Stardust	851	cutting	1957-71
Starflower	345	plate etching	1952-58; c61
Stars	110	cutting	1913-25
Stars	14	carving	37-60
Stars and Bars	47	carving	1941-47
Star Song	871	cutting	1959-66
Staunton	707	cutting	1933-44
Sterling	141	pressed	1888
Stockholm	6093 line	blown	1960-69
Stockholm	879	cutting	1960-69
Stowe	2862 line	pressed	1974-82
Stratford	914	cutting	1967-69
Stratton	2885 line	pressed	1970s-85; re
Strawberry Diamond & Fan			1904-13
Suffolk	789	cutting	1939-60
Sunflower	139	cutting	1920s
Sunglow	650	decoration	1960-68
Sunray	2510 line	pressed	1935-44
Sun Valley	15	crystal print	37-60
Sweetbrier	857	cutting	1958-60; c61
Sweetheart Rose	877	cutting	1960-75

Shirley

Shooting Stars

Silver Spruce

Skyflower

Skylark

Spinet

Spire

Spray

Spring

Spring Song

Springtime

Sprite

Stardust

Starflower

Star Song

Stratton

Sweetbrier

Sweetheart Rose

Swirl

Sylvan

Tara

Thistle

Transition

Trellis

True Love

Twilight

Valencia (Frosted Artichoke)

Victoria

Virginia

Name	Line/Number	Type	Dates
Swirl	848	cutting	1956-66
Sydney	1333 line	pressed	1905-13
Sylvan	1	crystal print	1955-66
Sylvan	1119 line	pressed	1902-06
Symphony	6065 line	blown	1956-68
Tapestry	701	cutting	1930-31
Tara	TA 01	crystal print	76-86
Tara	34	plate etching	1974-83
Tea Room (Colonial)	2222 line	pressed	1928-32
Tea Room Service	2460 line	pressed	37-60
Tempo	6032 line	blown	1942-44
Tenderness	691	decoration	1972-78
Terrace		tumblers	
Thelma	186	cutting	1928-29
Thistle	346	plate etching	1953-71
Thistle without band	202 1/2	plate etching	1904-10
Thoroughbred	40	carving	1940-44
Three Geese	26	carving	1940-44
Tiara	903	cutting	1964-71
Tiara	6044 line	blown	1950s
Tiger Lily	18	carving	37-60
Toy	620	decoration	1940-44
Toy	33	carving	1940-44
Transition	2936 line	pressed	1978-86
Trellis	822	cutting	1950-55; c61
Trellis	169	cutting	1924-28
Trojan	280	plate etching	1929-44
Trousseau	642	decoration	1958-79
True Love	862	cutting	1958-68
Tulip	772	cutting	1937-44
Tuxedo	1578 line	pressed	1908-10
Twilight	883	cutting	1960-63
U.S.A. Map	44	carving	1941-44
Vale	2863/925	cutting	1974-75
Valencia (Frosted Artichoke)	205	pressed	1891
Valentine Bells		cutting	76-86
Vase and Scroll	37	decoration	1924-30
Vendome	225	pressed	1891
Venise	688	decoration	1970-75
Venture	6114 line	blown	1969-71
Venus	896	cutting	1963-75
Vermeil	661	decoration	1965-78
Vernon	277	plate etching	1927-34
Verona	200	pressed	1891
Verona	281	plate etching	1929-32
Versailles	6113 line	blown	1969-73
Versailles	683	decoration	1969-72
Versailles	278	plate etching	1928-44
Vesper	6086 line	blown	1959-65
Vesper	275	plate etching	1926-34
Victoria	696	decoration	1965-85;1980-83
Victoria	6068 1/2 line	blown	1957-71
Victoria	183	pressed	1890
Victoria (Paradise)	71	decoration	1927-30
Victorian	4024 line	blown	1934-43
Victory	257	plate etching	1922-29
Viennese	506	decoration	28-37
Vigilant	403	pressed	1888
Viking	2563 line	pressed	37-60
Vintage	2713 line	pressed	37-60; 1961-65
Vintage	347	plate etching	37-60
Vintage	204	plate etching	1904-29
Virginia	2977 line	pressed	1978-85
Virginia	267	plate etching	1923-29
Virginia	1467 line	pressed	1906-15; re1969
Virginia (Captain Kidd)	140	pressed	1888
Vision	3008 line	blown	37-60; 1972-73
Vogue	6099 line	blown	1960-76
Vogue	2106 line	pressed	1916-29
Wakefield	820	cutting	1942-72+
Warwick	198	cutting	1929-33
Washington	266	plate etching	1923-29
Waterbury	712	cutting	1933-44
Watercress	741	cutting	1934-44; c61

Light Blue

Wakefield

Watercress

Wedding Bells

Wentworth

Westminster

Whisper

Wildwood

Williamsburg

Willow

Willowmere

Winburn

Waterfowl	1	carving	1938-44
Wavecrest	6014 1/2	blown	1936
Waveland	57	decoration	20-29
Wavemere	6030 line	blown	37-60
Waves	3	carving	37-60
Wedding Bells	789	pressed	1900-03
Wedding Flower	920	cutting	1969-71
Wedding Ring	626	decoration	1953-82
Wellington	722	cutting	1933-43
Wentworth	802	cutting	1940-44; c61
Westchester	6012 line	blown	1936-70
Westminster	872	cutting	1959-73
Westminster	723	cutting	1933-39
Weylin	759	cutting	1936-39
Wheat (Fostoria)	837	cutting	1953-74
Wheat	760	cutting	1936-40
Whirlpool	730	cutting	1934-40
Whisper	875	cutting	1960-71
Wildflower		deep etching	1921-24
Wildflower	308	plate etching	1931-33
Wildwood	854	cutting	1957; c61
Williamsburg	874	cutting	1960-70
Willow	335	plate etching	1939-45; c61
Willowmere	333	plate etching	1939-71
Wilma	6016 line	blown	1936-83
Wimbledon	6126 line	blown	1970s-82
Winburn	1704	pressed	1961-65
Windfall	870	cutting	1958-63
Windsor	6049 line	blown	1952-65
Wing	189	cutting	22-29
Wistar (Betsy Ross)	2620 line	pressed	1941-44
Woodland	2921 line	pressed	1975-82
Woodland	264	plate etching	1922-29
Yachting	8	carving	1938-42
York	1118 line	pressed	1902-04
York	709	cutting	1933-44
York	2934 line	pressed	1979-83
	23	engraving	1904-14
	77	cutting	1904-14
	104	cutting	1908-21
	184	pressed	1890s
	195	pressed	1890s
	210	etching	1910-28
	212	etching	1910-28
	214	etching	1910-28
	215	etching	1910-28
	223	etching	1913-18
	272	pressed	1891
	279	pressed	1891
	299	pressed	1891
	794	pressed	1890s
	956 line	pressed	1901-03
	1166 line	pressed	1902
	1223 line	pressed	1902-04
	1231 line	pressed	1903-08
	1300 line	pressed	1904-06; re 1969
	1303 line	pressed	1904-2

Other categories of products:

animals
art glass
blanks
bookends
buffet serving
candleabra, candlesticks
centerpieces
commemoratives
crowns
desk items
figurines
fruit jars

garden center
hurricane lamps
ink wells
miscellaneous
paperweights
plates, bowls
refreshment sets
shakers
smoking accessories
vases, pitchers
vanity items
wood or brass/glass

Windfall

Woodland

York

956 line

Glossary

abrasion - powders and mechanical devices remove portions of the surface; engraving, cutting, and carving are decorating methods using abrasion.

acid - chemical treatment to alter and decorate the surface; frosting, etching, and deep etching use acid.

blank - plain piece of glass ready to be decorated.

bobache - glass ring placed (or attached) on a candlestick to catch wax and to hold hanging prisms.

carving - three-dimensional pattern deeply engraved in heavy glass using sandblasting method.

chemical polishing - acid mixture is used to dissolve a thin layer of glass.

crystal - term usually refers to chemical content of the glass (lead crystal), but at Fostoria it simply meant colorless.

cutting - grinding with an abrasive wheel to produce grooves or facets; the ground glass grooves are called grey cuts before being polished to produce brilliant cut crystal.

decorating lehr - low-temperature oven that provides the heat required for decorating techniques such as gilding and enameling.

deep etching - creates a raised pattern similar to plate etching, but in reverse: the design is etched into a plate; acid-resist wax is applied to the surface (including the interior to protect the fire polish); hydrofluoric acid removes the background.

enameling - enamel colors mixed with a binder are painted onto the cold glass, then reheated in a decorating lehr to fuse the design to the surface.

engraving - use of abrasive powder and oil on a small revolving copper wheel to decorate the surface.

fire polishing - removing tool marks and smoothing the surface by reheating with fire.

flint glass - glass made with fine silica derived from quartz; however, the English formula also included lead oxide, hence the terms flint glass and lead glass have been used synonymously, even if the glass contained only lead and not flint; also a nineteenth-century term for fine glass.

font - reservoir for holding oil in a lamp

free blown - glass is blown and shaped with hand tools but no mold is used.

frosting - matte finish produced by lightly etching the surface with chemicals or sandblasting.

gilding - gold, silver, or platinum mixed with flux and a binder make a metallic paint which is applied to the cold glass and reheated to fuse it to the surface.

grey cutting - rough cutting and smoothing stages are completed but left unpolished.

grinding - abrasive powders and polishing wheels used at high speeds to remove unwanted areas such as pontil marks.

iridescent glass - surface of the hot ware is exposed to vapors of metallic salts which produce a chemical change creating surface iridescence.

lime glass - contains bicarbonate of soda and lime but no lead and is, therefore, less expensive to make than lead glass.

matte - nonglossy surface usually created with acid.

mechanical polishing - lightly abrasive powders and polishing wheels are used at slower speeds than for grinding.

milk glass - opaque milky white glass; colored opaque glass made in the same patterns is also loosely termed milk glass.

mold blown (also mould blown) - glass is blown into a wood or metal mold to give it shape and surface decoration.

mold mark - seam or raised line on the glass from the mold joint.

nappy - small dish (usually of glass) with a flat bottom and sloping sides used for serving food.

needle etching - blank is coated with acid-resist wax; design is drawn with a stylus through the wax; piece is dipped in hydrofluoric acid which etches the design onto the exposed glass. In production, needle etching is done on an assembly line with one operator controlling several concurrent mechanized etchings with a series of styluses. This method is faster and cheaper than plate etching but loses line crispness due to the jerky motion of the tracer and stylus. (Saffel)

off-hand - see free blown.

opalescent - portions of a pattern or edges of the glass turn a pearly opal white; this is caused when heat-sensitive calcium phosphate, which has been added to the glass batch, activates when the glass is reheated.

pattern mold - mold used for pattern only rather than shape.

plate etching - drawing is photo-engraved onto a steel plate .003-.0035 in. deep; drawing is coated with acid-resist wax and scraped off level with the plate (background); wax pattern is lifted with printer's paper and applied to the glass; piece is covered with wax except for the pattern, then dipped into hydrofluoric acid. (Saffel) This method replaced needle etching at Fostoria in the 1940s.

polishing - smoothing the surface by fire, chemicals, or abrasion.

pontil mark - rough (unless it is ground smooth) mark left at the bottom of a blown piece of glass after it has been broken off of the pontil rod (also called punty).

pressing - molten glass is poured into a patterned mold, usually of cast iron, which forms the decorated outer surface, and a plunger is pressed into the mass to create a smooth center or interior.

sand blasting - glass is bombarded with grit (sand) which removes the surface for some etching and deep carving techniques; the surface becomes translucent and rough.

silver deposit - .999 fine silver applied by electro-deposit method to create intricate designs.

soda lime glass - glass which contains soda as the main flux material.

Select Bibliography

Publications on Fostoria consisting primarily of catalog reprints:

Kerr, Ann. *Fostoria: an Identification and Value Guide.* Paducah, KY: Collector Books, 1994.

Litman, William and Lyla . *Fostoria No. 2056 American Pattern.* Fostoria Glass Society of America, 1986, reprinted 1989.

——.*Fostoria No. 2412 Colony Pattern.* Fostoria Glass Society of America, 1990.

Long, Milbra and Emily Seate. *Jamestown Pattern No. 2719.* 1992.

Mc Grain, Patrick H. *Fostoria: the Popular Years.* 1982.

Stinson, Ronald and Sunny. *Coin Glass Handcrafted by Fostoria 1958-1982.* Fostoria Glass Society of North Texas, 1988.

Weatherman, Hazel Marie. *Fostoria: the First Fifty Years.* Springfield, Missouri, 1972.

Reprints of some Fostoria trade catalogs have been available from the Fostoria Glass Society of America in Moundsville, West Virginia.

The microfiche collection of the Corning Museum of Glass contains Fostoria catalogs from 1890-1980, which are listed in *Guide to Trade Catalogs from the Corning Museum of Glass.* New York: Clearwater Publishing, 1987. Additional lists compiled by the museum are also available.

Catalogs and brochures most useful in this book were 1901, 1961, 1979, and 1982.

Publications with information and illustrations other than catalog pages:

Adt, Barbara. "Artist-Engineer: Phillip Ebeling." *Facets of Fostoria* Vol. XIV, No. 1, July 1993: 13-15.

——. "Artist-Engineer: Phillip Ebeling." *Facets of Fostoria* Vol. XIV, No. 4, Dec. 1993: 11-13.

Conley, Phil. "Fostoria – Magic Glassware: A Little Journey to a Big Industry." *The West Virginia Review*, Dec. 1927, reprinted in *Facets of Fostoria*, Vol. 13, Sept 1992: 4-8.

Eige, Eason. *A Century of Glassmaking in West Virginia.* Huntington: Huntington Galleries, 1980.

Falk, Peter Hastings, ed. *Who Was Who in American Art.* Madison Conn.: Sound View Press, 1985.

Florence, Gene. *Elegant Glassware of the Depression Era.* 5th ed. Paducah KY: Collector Books, 1993.

——.*Collectible Glassware from the 40s, 50s, & 60s.* Paducah KY: Collector Books, 1992.

Garmon, Lee. "Fostoria Coin Glass." *Glass Collector's Digest,* June/July 1989: 87-91.

Kamm, Minnie E. W. *Two Hundred Pattern Glass Pitchers.* Fifth ed., Watkins Glenn, N. Y.:Century House, 1956.

——. *A Second Two Hundred Pattern Glass Pitchers.* Third ed., Watkins Glen: Century House, 1956.

——. *A Third Two Hundred Pattern Glass Pitchers.* Detroit, 1953.

——. *A Fourth Pitcher Book.* Privately printed, 1950.

——. *A Fifth Pitcher Book.* Second ed., Privately printed, 1952.

——. *A Sixth Pitcher Book.* Second ed., Privately printed, 1954.

——. *A Seventh Pitcher Book.* Privately printed, 1953.

——. *An Eighth Pitcher Book.* Privately printed, 1954.

——. *The Kamm-Wood Encyclopedia of Antique Pattern Glass.* Volumes 1 and 2. Watkins Glen, New York: Century House, 1961.

Kerr, J. M. *Fostoria City Directory for 1889 and 1890.* Fostoria, Ohio, 1888.

Liebmann, Henry J. *Fostoria Factories: a History of the Factories of the Fostoria Glass Company.* 1991.

Long, Milbra A. *Fostoria Glass 1887-1986: A Guide for Study.* 1990.

Long, Milbra and Emily Seate. *Fostoria Stemware: The Crystal for America. Paducah KY: Collector Books, 1994.*

Murray, Melvin L. *History of Fostoria Ohio Glass 1887-1920.* 1972.

——. *Fostoria, Ohio Glass II.* 1992.

Pulos, Arthur J. *The American Design Adventure 1940-1975.* Cambridge: MIT Press, 1988.

Revi, Albert Christian. *American Pressed Glass and Figure Bottles.* New York: Thomas Nelson & Sons, 1964.

——. "The Fostoria Glass Company's Fancy Glass Lighting." *Spinning Wheel,* Oct. 1976: 31-33.

Saffell, Jon. "Fostoria Glass Company's Design Dept. - A History." *Facets of Fostoria.* 1983, Vol. II Nos. 1-5.

Seligson, Sidney P. *Fostoria American: a Complete Guide.* Wichita Falls, TX: 1993.

Thuro, Catherine M. V. *Oil Lamps: the Kerosene Era in North America.* Des Moines: Wallace Homestead, 1976.

——. *Oil Lamps II: Glass Kerosene Lamps.* Toronto: Thorncliffe House, 1983.

Warner, Ian. "Art Decorated Vases and Mugs." *Glass Collector's Digest* Feb/Mar 1988: 18-23.

Welker, John and Elizabeith Welker. *Pressed Glass In America: Encyclopedia of the First Hundred Years 1825-1925.* Ivyland, PA: Antique Acres Press, 1985.

Ziegler, Roserita. "Fostoria's Designer Collection." *Glass Collector's Digest* Feb/Mar 1994: 69-77.

Journals and Newsletters

China, Glass, and Lamps. various issues between 1890 and 1900.

Crockery and Glass Journal. various issues between 1887 and 1900.

Pottery and Glassware Reporter. various issues between 1887 and 1894.

The Daze. marketplace for china, glass, and pottery.

Facets of Fostoria. Fostoria Glass Society of America. Index covering 1980-1990 compiled by Gary Schneider.

Personal interviews:

Kenneth Dalzell, New Martinsville, West Virginia, March , 1994.

Melvin Murray, Fostoria, Ohio, May 1993.

Jon Saffell, Glen Dale, West Virginia, March, 1994.

Price Guide

It is well known that supply and demand drives prices. After nearly a century of production, it would seem then that Fostoria glass would be common and inexpensive. Yet many Fostoria patterns have become uncommon and expensive, because the only supply that has increased is the supply of collectors. As the market becomes driven by knowledgeable collectors and specialist dealers, prices standardize, especially for the most popular patterns. As with any dynamic market, prices also fluctuate, and actual ranges are often wider than any single price guide would indicate. Therefore, this or any guide should be consulted lightly and not be mistaken for a price list.

Dealers in various regions of the country create and follow trends independently of each other. Some may agree with the estimates in a guide; some may not. The purpose of a guide is to help its readers avoid making significant errors by being able to distinguish the common from the rare. If an item is estimated at $10-20, an example still might be found for $5, while another might be priced at $30. It would probably be unwise, however, to pay $200 for the item. As long as the guide is not taken too literally, and as long as the user realizes that prices are for items in perfect condition, that prices change, and that any guide will contain some errors, it should prove to be of some value. Naturally, the publisher cannot assume responsibility for any outcomes, yet wishes that all of your outcomes are good.

Prices for early pieces from Fostoria, Ohio are less reliable due to the rarity of most items. According to Mel Murray, the general desirability of patterns from most to least would probably be: Victoria as the most desirable, followed by Artichoke, Diamond Mirror, Ruth, Rococo and Late Icicle, Cascade and Verona, and lastly, Virginia, with only about one half the value of Victoria. For the American pattern, older items in colors are considerably rarer than crystal (or red) and are therefore more valuable. Any item made in Wisteria, a pastel lavender that changes under a black light, will be more valuable than the same item in any other color.

The following abbreviations are used: L=left; R= right; C=center; T=top; B=bottom; TL=top left; CL=center left; BL=bottom left; TC=top center; BC=bottom center; TR=top right; CR=center right; BR=bottom right.

Page	Photo	Position	Price
15	1.8		150-250
16	1.9	C	75-125
		L & R	60-120 pair
	1.10		50-60
17	1.12		50-75 each
	1.13		40-60 each
	1.14		60-90 each
18	1.15		50-75
	1.16		100-200
	1.17		60-100
	1.18		40-80 each
19	1.19		40-60 each
	1.20		75-125

Page	Photo	Position	Price
	1.21		50-75 each
20	1.22	L & R	50-75 each
		C	40-60
	1.23		50-75
	1.24		40-60 each
21	1.25		75-125
	1.26		80-120
	1.27		75-125
22	1.28		40-60 each
	1.29		20-40 each
	1.30		30-50 each
	1.31		30-50 each
	1.32		30-50 each
23	1.33		40-60 each
	1.34		75-125
24	1.36		50-75 each

Page	Photo	Position	Price
	1.37	L & R	50-75 each
		C	60-90
	1.38		75-125
25	1.39		60-80
	1.40	L & R	50-75 each
		C	20-40
	1.41		50-75 each
	1.42		75-125
26	1.43	T	60-80
		B	30-50
	1.44		75-125
	1.45	C	100-150
		L & R	60-80
27	1.46	L	60-90
		C	100-150
		R	60-90

No.	Ref	Pos	Value
	1.47	L	80-120
		C	50-75
		R	60-90
	1.48	L	80-120
		C	60-90
		R	40-60
28	1.49		175-225
	1.50	L	60-80
		C	60-80
		R	100-150
	1.51		100-150
	1.52		100-200
29	1.53		100-150
	1.54	L	60-90
		C	150-200
		R	75-100
	1.55	L	30-50
		TL	75-100
		BC	90-130
		R	50-75
30	1.56	T	100-150
		B	80-120
	1.57	L	60-90
		C	100-150
		R	40-60
	1.58		100-150 each
31	1.60	L	60-90
		R	100-150
	1.61		40-60 each
	1.62	L	60-90
		R	100-150
32	163		75-125
	1.64		40-60 each
	1.65		125-175
33	1.66	L	75-125
		C	90-130
		R	100-150
	1.67	L	60-90
		R	75-100
34	1.68	L	90-120
		TC	100-125
		BC	40-60
		R	60-90
	1.69		40-60
	1.70		40-60
35	1.71		75-100
36	1.73		75-125 each
	1.74	L	50-75
		C	60-90
		R	60-90
	1.75	L	40-60
		TC	75-125
		BC	30-50

No.	Ref	Pos	Value
		R	60-90
37	1.76		100-150
	1.77		80-120
	1.78	L	75-100
		R	20-40
38	1.79		200-300 each
	1.80		200-300
39	1.81		125-200
	1.82		150-250
40	1.83		150-250
	1.84		250-400
	1.85		150-250
	1.86		300-600
41	1.87		300-600
	1.88		300-600
	1.89		300-600
48	2.7	L	20-35
		R	25-40
49	2.9	T	10-15
		B	15-25
	2.10		30-50
	2.11	T	45-75
50	2.12		35-50
	2.13		300-400
51	2.14		75-125
	2.15		25-40
	2.16		30-40
52	2.17		300-400
	2.18		30-60
	2.19		75-150
53	2.20		70-120-
	2.22	L	50-75 complete
		R	20-40
54	2.23	L	25-50
		R	25-50
	2.24		10-20 each
	2.25	L	300-400
		R	75-150
	2.26		250-400 set
55	2.27	L	100-150
		CL	200-300
		R	50-100 set
	2.28		95-125
	2.29	L	25-50
		R	20-30 set
	2.30		40-60 each
56	2.31	L	50-75
		R	50-100
	2.32		10-20 each
	2.33	L	10-20
		R	20-40
	2.34	L	10-20

No.	Ref	Pos	Value
		R	20-40
	2.35		10-20 each
57	2.36		500+
58	2.37		1500-2000
59	2.38		250-350 old
			40-60 new
	2.39		200-300 set
	2.40		250-350 set
60	2.41	L	300-400
		R	300-400
	2.42	TL	80-120
		TR	300-400
		B	80-120
61	2.43	L	200-300
		C	300-350
		R	75-100
	2.44		100-125 each
62	2.45		1000+
63	2.46	L	250-350
		R	100-200
	2.47		100-200
64	2.48	TL	60-100
		BL	30-60
		TR	100-200
		BR	30-60
	2.49	L	50-100
		C	30-60
		R	75-125
65	2.52	L	30-80
		TR	100-200
	2.53	L	25-50
		R	10-15
	2.54		20-30 pair
	2.55		20-30
	2.56		30-50
67	2.61		40-60 each
	2.62		30-50
68	2.63	L	30-60
		C	30-60
		R	100-150
	2.64	L	100-150
	2.65	L	100-150
		R	40-60
	2.66	L	60-100
		C	100-150
		R	100-150
69	2.67		15-25
	2.68		10-15 each
	2.69		15-25
70	2.70		15-25 each
	2.71		15-25 each

No.	Figure	Position	Price
	2.72		25-40 each
	2.73	L	25-40
		C	50-75
		R	15-25
73	3.2		100-150 set
	3.3	L	50-70
		C	60-90
		R	80-100
74	3.4	C	75-125
		L & R	75-100 pair
	3.5	C	75-100
		L & R	75-100 pair
75	3.6		75-125
	3.7	L	40-70
		C	40-60 pair
		R	25-50
76	3.8		90-140
	3.9	L	70-100
		C	30-50
		R	40-60
77	3.10		70-90
78	3.12	L	25-45
		C	60-80
		R	15-20
	3.13	L	30-50
		LC	20-30
		RC	20-30
		R	25-50
79	3.14		50-70
	3.15	L	60-80
		R	30-50
80	3.16	L	150-200
		R	75-125
	3.17	L	75-125
81	3.18	L	60-80
		C	35-50
		R	40-60
	3.19	TL	20-40
		TR	60-80
		B	40-50 pair
82	3.20	L	30-40
		C	20-40 pair
		R	15-25
	3.21		40-60
83	3.22	C	30-50
		L & R	30-50 pair
	3.23	C	30-50
		L & R	40-60 pair
84	3.24	L	50-70
		CL	15-25
		CR	50-70
		R	15-25
	3.25		20-30 each
85	3.26		20-35 each
	3.27		30-50 each
	3.28	L	30-50
		R	20-30
86	3.29		50-60
87	3.32	L	75-100
		C	25-40
		R	50-75
	3.33		80-120
88	3.34	L	30-40
		C	150-250
		R	50-75 pair
	3.35	L	40-60
		C	15-25
		R	70-90
89	3.37	L	75-100
		C	40-60
		R	80-100
	3.38		25-35 each
92	4.4	C	75-100
		L & R	30-50 pair
93	4.6	L	20-30
		CL	20-30
		CR	75-100
		R	15-25
	4.7	C	100-150
		L & R	30-50 pair
	4.8	T	5-8
		B	25-40
94	4.9	L	15-20
		TR	100-150
		B	15-25 pair
	4.10		15-30 each
95	4.11	T	5-8
		B	40-50
	4.12		25-40
96	4.13	L	15-25
		C	100-150
		R	15-20
	4.14		20-30
97	4.16		80-120
	4.17	L	50-70
		C	80-120
		R	80-120
98	4.19		50-100
	4.20		40-80
99	4.21		60-90
	4.22		60-90
100	4.23		80-120
	4.24	L	50-75
		C	25-40
		R	30-60 pair
101	4.25		60-80
	4.26		60-80
102	4.28		30-60 pair
	4.29		60-90
103	4.30		125-200
104	4.32		20-40 each
		BC	40-50
	4.33	L	30-40
		C	15-25
		R	15-25
106	4.36		20-40 each
	4.37		50-70
	4.38		30-50 pair
	4.39		50-70
108	4.43		20-30 each
		BR	40-50
	4.44	L	20-30
		R	15-25
109	4.45		15-20 each
	4.46		80-120 pair
110	4.47	L	30-50 pair
		C	70-90 pair
		R	30-40 pair
	4.48	L	100-125 pair
		C	60-90 pair
		R	40-60 pair
	4.49		70-90
111	4.50		25-45
	4.51		30-50
	4.52		30-50
	4.53		25-45
112	4.54		20-35 each
	4.55		15-25 each
	4.56		20-25 each
114	5.3		75-125
115	5.5		100-150
116	5.7		50-75
117	5.8		100-150
118	5.9	L	60-90
		R	30-50
	5.11		15-25
119	5.12		75-100
120	5.15	L	40-60
		C	40-60
		R	75-100
	5.16	L	25-40
		CL	25-40
		CR	25-40
		R	40-60
121	5.17		15-25
	5.18		60-90
	5.19		40-60 each
122	5.20		100-150
	5.21		100-150
123	5.22		75-125

Page	Fig.	Pos.	Value
	5.23		60-90
125	5.29		40-60
	5.30	L	25-35
		C	15-30
		R	15-25
126	5.31		60-80 set
	5.32		60-80 set
127	5.33	TL	20-30
		BL	10-20
		C	20-30
		R	20-25
	5.34		60-90
	5.35		15-25 each
128	5.36		15-25 each
	5.37		15-25 each
	5.38	L	15-20
		R	20-25
129	5.39		100-200 set
	5.40	L	15-25
		R	10-20
130	5.41		40-60
131	5.43		75-125 each
	5.44		25-40
	5.45		25-40
132	5.46	L	15-20
		R	20-30
	5.47		15-25 each wisteria 30-40
133	5.49		40-60
134	5.50	L	20-30
		C	30-40
		R	20-30
	5.51	T	40-60
		C	20-30 set
		B	15-25
	5.52	T	15-25
		BL	30-40
		BC	40-60
		R	30-40
135	5.53	L	50-60
		R	10-20
	5.54	L	15-25
		R	25-35
	5.55	L	50-70 pair
		R	25-40 pair
136	5.56	L	30-40 each
		R	20-30 each
	5.57		30-50 pair
	5.58		60-90 pair
138	5.61	L	20-25 each
		R	70-100
139	5.62	L	25-35

Page	Fig.	Pos.	Value
		R	30-50
	5.63	L	20-30
		R	15-20 pair
	5.64		15-25
	5.65		15-25
140	5.66		75-100
	5.67	L	30-40
		C	15-25
		R	30-60
	5.68	L	40-60
		R	20-30
141	5.69		10-20 each
	5.70		10-20 each
	5.71		10-20 each
142	5.72		40-50
	5.73		20-30
	5.74		30-40
	5.75		30-60 set
143	5.76	L	50-60 each
		R	20-30 each
	5.77		25-35 pair
	5.78	L	20-25
		R	15-20
	5.79		15-20
144	5.80		15-20 each
	5.81		25-50
	5.83		40-60
145	5.84		50-70
	5.85		25-40 pair
	5.86	L	20-30
		R	100-150
146	5.87		100-150
	5.89		60-80
	5.90	T	100-150
		L	60-80
		R	80-120
147	5.91-5.95		15-20 each
149	5.98		10-15 each
150	5.99		10-25 each
	5.100		20-40 pair
	5.101	L	30-40
		R	40-50
151	5.103		15-20 each
152	5.104		20-30 each
	5.105		10-20
	5.106		15-30 each
153	5.109		10-15
	5.110		20-40
154	5.111		200-300
	5.112		75-125
	5.113	L & R	15-25 each
	5.114		15-25 each
155	5.115		20-25 each
	5.117		10-15 each

Page	Fig.	Pos.	Value
156	6.1		50-75 pair
157	6.2a &b		40-60 each
	6.3	L	25-50
		C	25-40
		R	25-40
158	6.4	L	40-60
		C	25-40
		R	25-40
	6.5		40-60
	6.6		50-70
159	6.7		25-40 each
	6.8		8-12 each
160	6.10		60-90
	6.11	L	50-75
		R	125-175
161	6.12		15-20 each
	6.13		15-20 each
	6.15		50-75
162	6.16		15-25
	6.17	L	20-30
		R	15-25
163	6.18		15-25
	6.19		15-25 each
	6.20	L	15-25
		R	50-75
164	6.21		40-60
165	6.23		40-60
	6.24		40-60
	6.25		40-60
166	6.26		30-50
	6.27		50-75
167	6.28		50-75
	6.29		25-35
	6.30		25-35
168	6.31		50-75
	6.32	L	20-30
		C	30-50
		R	20-25
169	6.33		20-25 each
	6.34	T	30-50
		B	40-60
170	6.37		20-30 each
	6.38		20-30 each
171	6.39	L	40-60
		C	30-50
		R	40-50
	6.40		25-40
175	6.49	L	10-15
		R	15-20
	6.50	L	15-20
		C	10-15
		R	15-20
	6.52		10-20 each

Index

For an alphabetical list of patterns and decorations in addition to those in the text, see Patterns and Decorations, 177-190.

A

Alexis, 125
Alvarez, Fernando, 8
American, 7, 8, 42-68
American Lady, 70
American Milestones, 8, 9
American States plates, 8, 153
American Whitehall, 42, 69
Animal Series, 8
Argus, 7, 148, 151-52
"Art Decorated" vases, 123
Art Deco vases, 10, 159
Artichoke, 6, 32-34, 38-40
Atlanta, 117
Avon, 71, 153

B

Baccarat, 7, 14
Baccarat Deposée, 7
Baroque, 7, 10, 133-36
Beaded Flange, 6
Beam, Charles E., 6, 7, 115
Belmont Glass Co., 6
Betsy Ross, 147
Bottome, Edgar, 6, 7, 8, 104
Bouquet, 111
Bradford, William, 9
Brady, William S., 6
Bridal Wreath, 111

C

Camellia, 110
Captain Kidd, 6, 22
Carpenter, James, 11
Cascade, 6, 14-18, 41
Central Glass Co., 71

Century, 8, 111, 137-39
Christmas ornament series, 8
Classic, 10
Cocanhougher, Robert, 8
Coin, 7, 71-89
Colonial, 8, 71
Colonial Dame, 143
Colony, 10, 140-143
Contrast, 171
Corsage Plum, 11
Crimmel family, 6
Crown collection, 10
Cupid, 103

D

Dalzell, David Beaty, 6
Dalzell, Harry G., 131
Dalzell, Kenneth, 6, 8, 42
Dalzell-Viking, 42, 71
Dalzell, William Alexander Baxter, 6
Dalzell, William F., 6
Designer collection, 11
Diamond Mirror, 36-37
Distinction, 8, 155

E

Ebeling, Phillip, 7, 8, 42, 120-21
Envoy, 10
Essex, 71

F

Facets, 11
Fairfax, 128
Fairmont, 10
Family paperweights, 11
Flame, 7, 136
Flemish, 8, 121
Foster Block (see Virginia)
Foster, Charles, 6
Fostoria Barrel and Stave Co., 15

Fostoria Glass Co. stock certificate, 13
Fostoria Glass Society of America, 125, 154
Fostoria, Ohio, 5
Fostoria Ohio Glass Association, 13
Fostoria Ruby, 6
Fostoria Swirl, 6, 25-26
Frosted Artichoke, (see Artichoke)

G

Gourmet, 11
Grace, 8
Grape, 97-101
Greenfield, 9
Grove, Robert, 9

H

Hannum, Robert F., 6
Hartford, 120
Heirloom, 163-67
Henry Ford Musuem, 151
Heritage, 8, 155
Heritage Gallery, 13, 14
Hermitage, 132
Hobbs, Brockunier & Co., 6
Hoffer, William, 9
Holly, 111-12
Homespun, 163
Humperville, Harry, 6
Huntington Museum of Art, 113-14

I

Icicle (see Late Icicle)
Indiana Glass Co. 42
Indiana Tumbler and Goblet Co., 7
Iroquois China, 11
Isaac Harter Co., 15

J

Jaeger, Otto, 6
Jamestown, 10, 148-50
Jenny Lind, 145-46
June, 7, 104-05

K

Karnak, 175
Kokomo Glass Co., 7
Kopp, Nicolas, 6

L

Labels, 176
Lafayette, 127
Lancaster Colony Corp., 6, 7, 42, 71
Late Icicle (Icicle), 6, 23-25, 39
Lenox Glass, 7
Lido, 135
Loewy, Raymond, 10
Long Buttress, 71, 122
Lorraine, 6, 37
Lotus, 169-70
Louise, 120
Lucere, 121

M

Madonna, 134
Magee, William H., 8
Mah Jongg Sets, 126
Marguerite, 6
Martin, Lucien B., 6, 7
Mayfair, 158-59
Maypole, 144
Meadow Rose, 110
Melissa, 8
Mesa, 8
Module, 11
Monarch, 11
Monroe, 144-145
Moonmist, 168
Moonstone, 8, 148
Morgantown Glass Guild, 6
Moundsville, West Virginia, 6

N

National Glass Co., 6
Navarre, 7, 107-08
Needlepoint, 162
Neo Classic, 171
New Garland, 7

O

Oak Leaf, 97, 100-02
Old Glory, 8
Olert, Judy, 9
Olive, 6
O'Neal, Hayes, 6

P

Panelled Diamond Point, 9
Paradise, 97-98
Pebble Beach, 11
Pettit, Greg, 9
Pioneer, 94
Precedence, 11
Pressed No. 184, 30-31; No. 195, 31; No. 272, 35; No. 504, 120; No. 794, 114-15; No. 1660, 120
Pricilla, 157

Q

Queen Anne, 12

R

Radiance, 10
Regal, 152
Revere, 8
Riihimáki, 11
Robin Hood, 118
Rococo, 6, 34
Roe, Calvin B., 6
Romance, 108-10
Roulette, 168
Royal, 92-96
Russel, J. B., 6
Ruth, 6

S

Saffell, Jon, 8, 9, 11, 154
St. Bernard, 115-16
St. Francis, 154
Sakier George, 7, 8, 9-10, 149, 159
Salem, 8
Scroggins, Deacon, 6
Seascape, 168-69
Seashells, 11, 171

Seibel, Ben, 11
Seneca Glass Co., 6
Serendipity, 11
Seville, 110
Sheraton, 8
Society of Industrial Designers (SID), 10
Sorrento, 10
Spencerian O, 90
Spinet, 161
Sterling, 6, 23
Steuben, 11
Stratton, 8
Sun Ray, 129-130

T

Transition, 9
Trojan, 7
Tut vase, 157
Tynell, Helena, 11, 171

V

Valencia (see Artichoke)
Vanity set, 131
Vendome, 6
Vernon, 7
Verona, 6, 31
Versailles (blown), 10
Versailles (etching), 6, 104-06, 120
Victoria, 6, 7, 14, 26-30, 41
Viking Glass, 7
Virginia, 6, 18-22, 38, 40
Virginia (later), 148
Vogue, 8
Voitle, J. F., 6

W

Wheeling, West Virginia, 5
Whirlpool, 10, 161
Wright, Russel, 10, 172

Y

Yehl, Fred, 9
York, 11
Yutzey, Marvin, 8